Scarborough Castle

John Goodall

CONTENTS

Tour of the Castle

THE SETTING

From the ticket office, it is possible to appreciate the natural drama of the Scarborough headland. The castle occupies the tip of one in a series of promontories that project into the North Sea along this stretch of the Yorkshire coast. The diamond-shaped plateau of land on which it sits is comprised of horizontal beds of Jurassic limestone and sandstone. These form high cliffs on the three seaward sides of the headland. On the fourth, the rock has been eroded, creating a steep slope that drops towards the town. The natural fall of the land on this side of the headland has been artificially accentuated to form a massive double ditch. The ticket office stands on a narrow causeway created by a geological fault that spans one end of the ditch. It forms the only approach to the castle. On either side of the headland are broad bays. The one to the south is sheltered and has long been used as a harbour. Protected from the prevailing winds and with a sandy shore well-suited for landing boats, it has been crucial to the prosperity of Scarborough since the Iron Age. This headland site has been intermittently occupied for nearly 3,000 years.

Above: An aerial view of the Scarborough headland from the south, showing the harbour

Facing page: A visitor speaks to a local woman beneath the great tower in a photograph of the 1890s

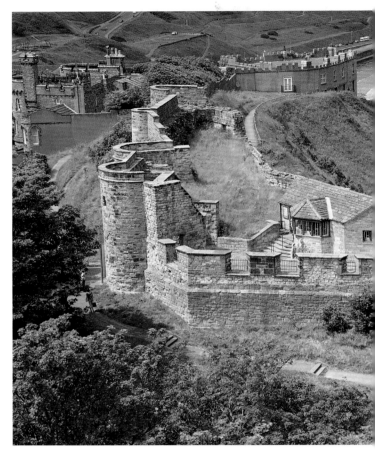

∎ BARBICAN AND GATE

The path from the ticket office to the great tower is the natural causeway to the headland, and it was formidably defended in the Middle Ages as a barbican or outer fortification to the castle. Surrounding the ticket office is a fortified enclosure with its own towers and gatehouse. From this point upwards the path was once enclosed within walls 5.5m (18ft) high, which supported wall-walks that allowed the garrison to overlook the ditch on either side.

Right: The barbican gate, although much rebuilt, probably reflects the form of an original built in about 1300. An oddly shaped fragment of stone in the left-hand tower is all that remains of a carved shield bearing the royal arms in a form current from 1405

Above: A 13th-century miniature of Henry III, who built the barbican gate tower and bridge between 1243 and 1245

Left: A view of the barbican showing the main gate to the left and the bridge to the right

Below: A 19th-century engraving showing the barbican bridge. At that time one of the drawbridges still operated

About halfway up the causeway, the path was interrupted by a fortified bridge with two drawbridges. These were set on either side of a gate tower that stood on the central pier of the bridge, and each was closed with its own portcullis. Clustered around the gate tower at the outer corners of the drawbridge pits were four smaller turrets. The gate tower has now lost its upper storey and the drawbridge pits have been built over.

Extensive rebuilding makes it impossible to date the various medieval elements of the barbican with certainty. The first reference to a barbican occurs in 1175 and the foundations of a square tower, which possibly belongs to this 12th-century fortification, lie beneath the ticket office. Most of the existing features, however, are later in date. The barbican gate tower and bridge were built by Henry III (r.1216–72) between 1243 and 1245 and compare in design with the Black Tower at Newcastle and the 1280s entrance to Conwy Castle.

Entrance from the barbican into the main castle enclosure was through a gateway (now lost) called 'Constable Tower', set immediately beneath the great tower. Extending to either side of this gateway was a fortified wall – or curtain – which, from at least the early 13th century, encircled the entire headland. Only the part overlooking the town remains.

Above: The master gunner's house with its crow-step gables. There was once a garden to the rear of the building but over time it has collapsed down the cliff

Below: A training battery being dismantled at Scarborough on 8 January 1899, from The Navy and Army Illustrated. *The men in the photograph are not in uniform and may be local volunteers*

2 MASTER GUNNER'S HOUSE

This house, with its stepped gables and fine wooden stair, was probably converted from an existing building in the early 18th century as the lodging for a master gunner. It is one of the finer examples among others of this period – at Carlisle, Walmer and Dover castles and at the Garrison, St Mary's, on the Isles of Scilly. The building was altered before 1821, probably when the Ordnance Office created a larger establishment, with a storekeeper as well as a master gunner, during the Napoleonic Wars (1793–1815). A plan of 1821 shows a cellar, a parlour and kitchen on the ground floor, a pair of bedchambers on the first floor and three small attic rooms. Today, the house contains an exhibition on the history of the headland.

Scarborough's Master Gunners

Heavy guns were mounted in Scarborough Castle because of its strategic position on the East Coast shipping route. Long periods passed, however, without soldiers at Scarborough, the only permanent presence being the employees of the Ordnance Office. This body supplied equipment to the Army, built permanent fortifications, maintained coastal gun batteries and employed military engineers and gunners to build and man them. Coast batteries usually had a master gunner, plus one or two ordinary gunners. The master gunner was an experienced or veteran artilleryman who maintained the guns, shot, gunpowder and equipment needed for cleaning, firing and transport. In wartime, he and his gunners assisted an expanded garrison of regular and militia artillerymen; they also trained unskilled men and volunteers. This was necessary because Scarborough normally had between 8 and 20 guns, each of which needed on average four men to work efficiently.

A master gunner lived at Scarborough from at least 1652, at which time there were also eight gunners. A master gunner was still resident until at least 1844 and in later years there were usually no more than one or two gunners, their number boosted by militia or volunteers. The main group of guns was in South Steel Battery, overlooking the harbour, but in wartime others were positioned on the east and south, defending the approaches from the town. The type and number of guns varied over time but nearly all were smooth bores ('cannon') on truck or garrison carriages, though in the later 19th century there were also a few powerful rifled guns.

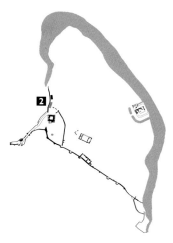

An inventory in 1661 listed 25 serviceable artillery pieces. These were mostly medium guns, the largest a 'culverin', firing a shot weighing 18 pounds (8.16kg), and the smallest a 3-pounder (1.36kg). There was also a stock of small arms for an infantry garrison, including 433 matchlock muskets and 490 long pikes. During the Napoleonic Wars, there were 15 18-pounders, capable of engaging warships that might threaten the harbour.

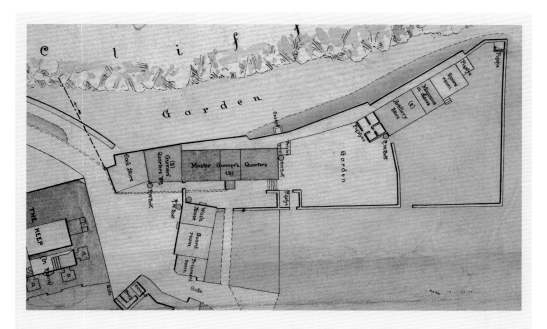

The Master Gunner

Master gunners were senior non-commissioned officers; at Scarborough the master gunner may also have acted as storekeeper for military supplies. His everyday life was comfortable and not too onerous, with a routine of cleaning and maintaining the guns, checking stores and looking after Ordnance buildings and property. On occasion, the guns would be tested and fired and sometimes moved.

This plan shows the buildings around the master gunner's house in 1879, most of which had been built before or during the Napoleonic Wars. The mix of military and domestic uses is clear from the annotations, with a garden and pigsties between the master gunner's house and the magazine and a store for artillery equipment to the north. Adjacent to the house there was a guardhouse and quarters for an additional gunner and a coal store.

Right: A section of a 15th-century cross-shaft, carved on its four principal sides. This side shows Christ on the cross flanked by the Virgin Mary and St John. It once formed part of a large cross from the chapel site

Below: A replica of a Bronze Age sword (1,000–700 BC), which was excavated from the site of the King's Hall in 1980

Below right: A medieval jet cross pendant

The Collections

Excavations at Scarborough have uncovered a wide range of artefacts spanning the whole period of the site's history. They give a fascinating glimpse of life on the headland over the past 3,000 years.

Tools and pottery dating from prehistoric times have been found, including a bronze axe-head (see page 23) and a magnificent Bronze Age sword.

Some Iron Age and Roman glass beads have been uncovered on the site of the Roman signal station (see page 24); they must once have formed part of necklaces or bracelets. A number of Roman pottery vessels, used to store, cook and serve food and drink, have also been discovered.

No Viking artefacts have been uncovered as yet at Scarborough. This medieval jet cross pendant, which was found in the graveyard of the chapel of Our Lady, is one of two such pendants excavated at the castle. Many of the later finds date from the time of the Civil War, when the castle was besieged. They include iron and stone shot (see page 34).

3 INNER BAILEY

The ditched enclosure that encircles the great tower was once walled and had two gates opening onto the headland. It has been possible to trace within the inner bailey the outlines of lost buildings by measuring variations in the resistance of the ground to an electric current – a technique known as resistivity. It appears that in the mid 12th century a courtyard of buildings on a regular plan existed on the site. One corner of this courtyard was demolished in the 1150s to make space for the great tower. Presumably, the surviving courtyard operated as ancillary structures to the great tower at this date.

Fragments of carved masonry likely to be from the 12th-century courtyard have been found re-used in King John's buildings in the castle, suggesting that John (r.1199–1216) demolished the remainder of the courtyard after he began remodelling the castle in 1202. As well as the lodgings and hall in the outer bailey, John built a second, additional hall. It is unclear as to why this second hall was built. It stood against the outer curtain wall at the southern corner of the inner bailey, next to one of the towers. Curiously, the foundations adjoining the hall are laid out to receive a D-shaped tower, but the building itself was actually polygonal in plan.

John's hall fell into ruin and was replaced by a kitchen, brewhouse and bakehouse in the 14th century. The remains of these, which include the base of an oven, can still be seen. There is also a well in the bailey, probably built in the 12th century. It is more than 46m (150ft) deep and the stone lining goes down 20.7m (68ft) before giving way to natural rock.

Aerial view of Scarborough Castle looking north

A *Inner bailey*
B *14th-century service buildings*
C *Great tower*
D *Site of gatehouse*
E *Site of King John's hall*
F *Curtain wall*
G *Well*
H *Base of oven*

Left: A view of the ruined great tower

A Forebuilding

B Site of the chapel

C First-floor chamber

D The second floor once comprised two chambers divided by a spine wall

Facing page: A reconstruction drawing of the great tower in about 1200

A Forebuilding

B Chapel

C First-floor chamber, which was probably a hall for the royal household

D The outer chamber of the second floor, which formed part of a set of inner apartments for the king. It appears to have a throne niche at one end of the room

E Latrine chutes

In addition to the main rooms in the tower, there were passages and chambers inside the walls. There was also a stair to the chapel in the forebuilding beside the entrance door. A broad spiral stair, connecting all the floors, rose up the lost western side of the tower, where its lowest steps still survive. In the wall beside it are the arched outlet chutes for latrines. It was common for latrines to be stacked one above the other in great towers. Presumably, therefore, the lost wall incorporated latrine chambers on each floor to either side of the stair well.

The uppermost storey of the tower was probably filled by the roof structure. This presumably explains why there are no wall chambers or fireplaces at this level. Curiously, it is impossible to identify seating for a roof in the main walls, but the central partition wall, on which the roof must have rested, clearly never extended above second-floor level.

No documents reveal how the tower was used in the 12th century. The large first-floor chamber was probably a hall for the royal household, while the second-floor chamber formed a set of inner apartments for the king. Of the two chambers on the second floor, the one entered from the main stair is likely to have been a public room, while that to the east was private and comfortably appointed. With two doorways between them the king could either invite visitors through to see him (through the grand door in the partition wall) or appear ceremonially at one end of the outer chamber.

The tower compares in certain technical details and planning to three earlier great towers at Bungay, Walden and Castle Hedingham, all in East Anglia. Perhaps the mason involved at Scarborough previously worked in this area.

Above: A view across the bay to the south of the headland

5 VIEWING PLATFORM

There is a fine view from here of the castle walls and ditches as well as a view of the town. The medieval town, enclosed by ditches and gates, extended across the full width of the promontory between the two bays and its medieval street plan is largely preserved.

Immediately below the castle is the parish church of St Mary, which was developed from the late 12th century on an unusually grand scale. The church was occupied as an outpost by Parliamentarian troops during the siege of 1645. In the course of the fighting its chancel was damaged and this part of the church is now a ruin. The central tower was rebuilt in 1669. To the left, along the line of the castle curtain wall, it is possible to appreciate the sheer scale of the outer ditch and the stone fortifications erected by King John. To the right is the fortified bridge erected by Henry III and the barbican beneath it. Beyond the castle is a fine and prominent group of 1860s buildings in a castellated Gothic style called 'The Towers' and 'The Castle-by-the-Sea'.

The view across the castle from the viewing platform is also impressive. The great tower is seen against the sea. To the right, in the distance, are the excavated remains of the Roman signal station and chapel. Also visible from here is the outline of the inner bailey, and just beyond it, the foundations of the great hall.

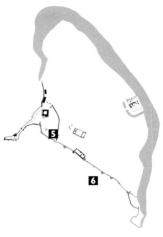

6 CURTAIN WALL

This surviving stretch of curtain wall that overlooks the town was built by King John between 1202 and 1212. It presumably replaced an earlier line of defences. There are two different types of tower along the wall. Within the inner bailey, the curtain wall towers are solid and have no internal chambers. In contrast, those in the section of the curtain wall that drops south to the cliff (except two turrets added in the 14th century) are hollow, to allow for the insertion of floors. This change suggests that the section around the inner bailey was built first. The break in construction possibly corresponds to the year 1206–7 when, for no apparent reason, the level of expenditure on the castle suddenly dropped. In the 1730s a cliff collapse damaged the Cockhyll Tower at the southern extreme of the curtain wall, and this is now lost.

Above: The line of the inner bailey wall erected by King John. The barbican walls were added later in the 13th century

Below: A crowd on the harbour pier watches a ship being broken on the rocks beneath the castle, in a watercolour of 1793 by Francis Nicholson. Clearly visible to the top left is the distinctive line of King John's main castle wall punctuated with towers

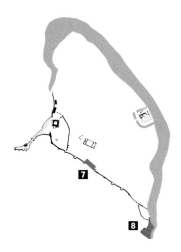

7 KING JOHN'S CHAMBER BLOCK

These ruins of a royal lodging, now known as Mosdale Hall, were under construction between 1210 and 1211 and form part of a residence – complete with a nearby hall and block of withdrawing apartments – in the outer bailey of the castle. It is not clear why King John thought it necessary to construct a residential complex at Scarborough when the castle already had a great tower. Perhaps the rooms in the great tower were reserved for ceremonial use and the residential complex was for the queen or the senior members of the royal household. It was common in the 12th century to create residences in castles beside great towers, though the reasons for doing so remain obscure.

Until the mid 13th century it was common for grand houses to have a separate kitchen, hall and chamber block. This was the case at Scarborough, and traced in the grass a short distance from King John's lodging are the foundations of the great hall it served.

The two-storey chamber block was divided by a partition wall to create one large and one small room on each level. A curtain wall tower constructed on a polygonal plan at the north corner of the block provided an extra room opening off each floor. At the opposite (south) end is a latrine pit.

Above: In its original form, King John's chamber block was a prominent feature of the castle. This detail from the 1538 survey shows it rising above the line of the curtain wall. Despite its appearance at this date, we know from documentary sources that the building was in decay

Below: Plan, section and elevation of the new barracks erected after 1745 within the chamber block. The officers' rooms were to the left and those of other ranks to the right

All that survives today of this building is its basement, lit by windows along both sides. The lost floor above was the principal storey, and its rooms perhaps connected with a chapel in the tower. Both upper rooms were warmed by fires (the stone bases that supported the hearths of these survive) and, to judge from the projecting stone foundations at either end of the building, had separate external stairs and porches. The existing foundations are later additions to the building but probably reflect earlier arrangements.

This lodging was still in use in 1260, during Henry III's reign, and also in 1361, when a survey made for Edward III (r.1327–77) describes the 'Queen's Chamber' as being located here. It then had three mud-wall buildings around it. A survey of 1538, however, indicates that the building was in ruins.

Soon after 1745 the lodging was converted into a barrack block. The medieval fabric was cased in brick and adapted to create a building on three floors with separate sections, corresponding to the ancient internal partition wall, for officers and other ranks. Badly damaged by German shelling in 1914, the barrack was demolished and the brickwork stripped away from all but the exterior of the curtain wall.

8 SALLY PORT AND SOUTH STEEL BATTERY

Just short of the present cliff edge, a small door or sally port passes through the curtain wall. Descending from it is a covered staircase set with musket loops, which leads to South Steel Battery. This gun emplacement was built by the town in 1643 to command the harbour. It was enlarged between 1652 and 1657, but it was probably not until 1745 that the sally port and staircase with musket loops were built. The battery remained in use into the 19th century, but part of it had collapsed by 1847. Further erosion has rendered it unstable.

Above: Members of the coastguard outside the bomb-damaged barracks in 1914, from Scarborough Pictorial, *6 January 1915*

Below: A view of the harbour and castle by Francis Place, 1701. The top half of the picture clearly shows the lost Cockhyll Tower and South Steel Battery

9 KING'S HALL

The great hall was a public chamber, where the whole household ate. It is set apart from the chamber block and follows the classic medieval form for such buildings. The roof was supported internally on two rows of wooden posts. One of the square stone bases for these posts survives and the positions of the remainder are shown in the grass.

At the low, or service, end of the hall, in this case towards the north-west, were three doorways, which may originally have been concealed from the main body of the room by a screen. That in the middle opened onto a corridor that led to the kitchen, while those on each side served a buttery and pantry chamber. The kitchen is not aligned with the hall and is set apart to reduce the risk of fire. The main entrance to the building was in a side wall, and it may also have been concealed behind a screen. In the 14th century the hall, described as 'King's Hall' in a survey of 1361, was divided in two by a wall that had an external buttress at either end.

Above: A view of the great tower and inner bailey across the footings of the King's Hall. The square stone base to the right supported a timber arcade post and the wall foundation aligned with it shows that the hall was at one time partitioned internally

Below: A 15th-century depiction of a feast in a great hall. The room is hung with rich fabrics and there is a display of plate on the dresser to the right

hus qui seruant testamentum eius.
t memores sunt mandatorum
ipsius : ipsius : ad faciendum ea.

Monarchs on the Move

Medieval kings were perpetually moving around, billeting themselves and their retinues either in royal manors and castles, or in those of their subjects. They took with them all their personal belongings, which were unpacked to furnish any building in which they stayed. In the early 12th century the king and his mobile household constituted the central organ of administration and rule. Gradually, however, departments of government – such as the exchequer – were permanently established in Westminster.

Although individual offices might be separate from the household, the monarch remained the centre of power and access to him was a vital element in securing political influence.

The extent, scale and purpose of royal progresses varied immensely between reigns, but in times of peace, it was typical for kings to visit a core of favourite residences with a relatively small household. Virtually without exception these core residences lay in the south-east of England and were associated with hunting parks. At times of political difficulty or war, however, progresses could go to every corner of the realm and involve very large numbers of people. King John is known to have visited Scarborough several times and seems to have developed it, along with Knaresborough, as a major royal castle to control Yorkshire.

> The monarch remained the centre of power and access to him was a vital element in securing political influence

Above: A depiction of a noble household on the move from the 14th-century Luttrell Psalter
Left: A late 14th-century leather costrel – a barrel-shaped travelling drink bottle, which could be carried on a cord on the belt or round the neck

Above right: A detail from the 1538 survey showing the well and chapel of Our Lady with a belfry tower
Below: A conjectural evolution of the signal station site in the Middle Ages

A 1000

B 12th century

C 13th century

D 1538

🔟 ROMAN SIGNAL STATION

When this area was excavated in the 1920s traces were found of three important phases of occupation. The earliest finds, of which nothing is now visible, were a series of Iron Age storage pits and post holes, dating to between 800 and 500 BC. Built across these were the remains of a fourth-century AD Roman signal station and various medieval foundations, including those of a chapel. It is the combined remains of the Roman and medieval structures that form the confusion of walls, mounds and ditches visible today.

To distinguish the details of the Roman signal station, trace the outline of the grass-covered mounds and dips. These consist of three square-planned Roman features set one within the other, parts of which have been lost over the cliff: working inwards there is a ditch, an enclosure wall and the base of a tower. Excavation revealed the bases for timber posts within the tower foundation, presumably supports for a floor, and also the bases of D-shaped towers at each corner of the enclosure wall. On the landward side of the signal station are the exposed foundations of a gateway, partly obscured by medieval walls.

There is much debate about the precise dating, appearance and function of this building, but its remains compare closely with similar fourth-century structures which survive, or are known to have existed, on the Yorkshire coast at Filey, Huntcliffe and Goldsborough. The likelihood is that it comprised a low-walled enclosure and a tall central tower with a beacon or lookout on top. How high this might have stood is a matter for speculation. The signal station was probably built in the 360s or 380s as one in a chain of lookout stations intended to warn of the approach of raiders.

CHAPEL OF OUR LADY

The exposed stone foundations remain incompletely understood. In about 1000 a chapel dedicated to Our Lady (the Virgin Mary) was built over the foundations of the Roman signal station **A**. The chapel was extended **B** in the 12th

century, and a domestic range to its north was built **C**, possibly in the 13th century (or perhaps even as late as the 16th century). By 1538, the chapel had been reduced in length and a freestanding tower was built beside it **D**. The chapel was associated with a well, 'Our Lady's Well'. The brick cistern seen in the vault is 18th century.

Aerial view (above) and plan (below) of the Roman signal station and medieval chapel

1 *Signal station ditch*
2 *Signal station enclosure wall*
3 *Square base of Roman tower*
4 *Medieval chapel walls*
5 *Well*

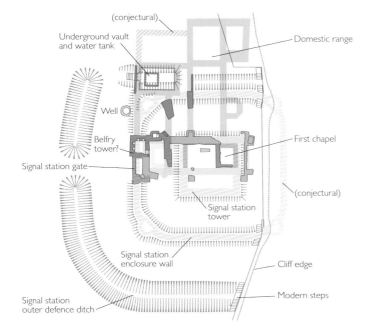

(conjectural)

Underground vault and water tank

Domestic range

Well

Belfry tower?

First chapel

Signal station gate

Signal station tower

(conjectural)

Signal station enclosure wall

Cliff edge

Signal station outer defence ditch

Modern steps

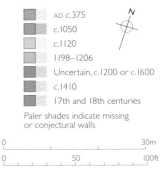

AD c.375
c.1050
c.1120
1198–1206
Uncertain, c.1200 or c.1600
c.1410
17th and 18th centuries

Paler shades indicate missing or conjectural walls

0   30m
0   50   100ft

History of the Castle

PREHISTORY

The earliest evidence of human activity on the promontory at Scarborough are fragments of Beaker pottery dating from between about 2,100 and 1,600 BC. But it is only in the first millennium BC that there is clear evidence of a settlement here. Excavations on the headland have revealed pits, post holes and a wide variety of prehistoric artefacts, including axe-heads, metalwork and pottery. These suggest two distinct periods of habitation, the first in about 800 BC and the second in about 500 BC. It is not clear how extensive either settlement was and sea erosion may have destroyed much evidence of both.

ROMAN SIGNAL STATION

The foundation of a new legionary fortress at York in AD 71 enabled the Romans to dominate the region north of the Humber. Coin finds in the harbour suggest that Roman ships anchored at Scarborough and archaeological excavations in the town have revealed evidence for the establishment of a farming settlement here by the late third century AD. Then, in the late fourth century, a tower, fortified with a wall and ditch, was erected on the headland.

Above: Bronze Age axe-head, c.1,000–700 BC, found in a pit on the headland
Below: A reconstruction of the Roman signal station with its tower, walls and ditch

Facing page: The natural harbour beneath the headland has underpinned Scarborough's prosperity since prehistory

Above: Coins found in the harbour at Scarborough suggest that this bay was used by Roman ships
Right: A Roman walled enclosure, on a scale and plan similar to that of the Scarborough signal station, survives at the Nunnery on Alderney in the Channel Islands
Below: Iron Age and Roman glass beads found on the site of the Roman signal station

It is likely that this building was one in a set of signal stations erected along the north-east coast of Britain at this time, because of its architectural similarity to other sites and similar finds of coins and pottery. Remains of closely comparable structures, with towers, enclosure walls and ditches, survive, or are known to have existed, at Filey, Huntcliffe and Goldsborough, all on the Yorkshire coast.

Until recently these signal stations were thought to have been built by Count Theodosius in response to the so-called 'Barbarian Conspiracy' of 367. In that year an orchestrated invasion of the Western Roman Empire by barbarian tribes brought imperial authority in Britain to the verge of collapse, and the emperor, Valentinian (r.364–75), sent Theodosius to restore order. After a successful campaign to secure imperial government, Theodosius was active in strengthening Britain's defences and it was assumed that these forts were part of this work. More recently, however, they have been attributed to Magnus Maximus, a usurping emperor, acclaimed by his troops, who ruled Britain between 383 and 388.

How the forts worked as signal stations is much debated. Some scholars think that they were part of a chain, extending right down the east coast from Hadrian's Wall, designed to watch for raiders and enabling ships and military units to intercept them. But since only four have been identified for certain, it has been necessary to infer the existence of several others, at places such as Whitby. One alternative suggestion is that the stations acted independently to warn inland settlements of attack.

Whatever purpose they served, it is generally supposed that the signal stations were abandoned in the early decades of the fifth century, at the end of Roman rule in Britain. There is no explicit proof for this at Scarborough but the evidence of archaeological excavations of the signal station at Filey would appear to corroborate this date.

SCARBOROUGH IN NORDIC SAGA

It has long been supposed that the name Scarborough derives from Old Norse and translates as 'the stronghold of Skardi' ('Skardi' means 'the man with the hare lip'). The principal evidence for the importance of Scarborough as a Viking centre comes from Icelandic sagas. Of particular significance is the description found in several sagas of an attack on Scarborough by the Norwegian king Harald Hardrada (r.1046–66) in 1066.

According to these accounts, Hardrada's fleet touched land north of Scarborough and then sailed down the coast towards it. After meeting stiff resistance from the inhabitants, Hardrada built a huge bonfire on the rock above the town and had burning brands thrown onto the houses beneath. His men then slew many of the inhabitants.

Unfortunately, the most detailed account of this attack, in the Codex Frisianus, was compiled in the 13th century, long after the events it purportedly records. Even more importantly, there is as yet no clear archaeological evidence for any Viking occupation in the area of the town. It may be that the sagas invented a Viking history for Scarborough, because the town later became so important.

As a result, the whole idea of a Viking settlement at Scarborough has recently been called into question. Moreover, an alternative Anglo-Saxon etymology for the name Scarborough as 'the hill with the fort' has also been suggested.

Whether Scarborough is of Viking or Anglo-Saxon origin, it is clear that there were people present on the headland by 1000. The 1920s excavation of the signal station revealed a chapel within the foundations of the central Roman tower, as well as a small cemetery. This building became the chapel of Our Lady in the later Middle Ages.

Above: The Last Voyage of the Vikings, *painted in 1882 by Robert Gibb. The Viking origins of Scarborough may be no more than Victorian fantasy*
Below: *Vikings in their long boats, from a 10th-century Scandinavian manuscript*

'Then put King Harald into Scarborough and fought there against the townsmen. He went up unto the mount there where it highest was and had made a great bonfire and set fire to it, but when the fire was blazing they took great forks and pushed it down into the town, so that all the houses set fire to one another and the town surrendered.' (Codex Frisianus, 13th century)

Above: Portrait of Henry II from the 'Flores Historiarum' by Matthew Paris, 1250–52. Henry built the great tower at Scarborough Castle between 1159 and 1169

Below: The great gatehouse, built in the 1380s, at Thornton Abbey, the foundation and burial place of William le Gros, who also founded Scarborough Castle in the 12th century

THE EARLY CASTLE

Scarborough is not mentioned in the Domesday survey of 1086, which suggests that no significant settlement existed here at that date. It is first clearly documented in the mid 12th century during the reign of Henry II (r.1154–89) as a borough prospering beneath the walls of a great royal castle. This was not, in fact, the first castle at Scarborough.

The founder of the castle was William le Gros, Count of Aumâle. He was created Earl of York by King Stephen (r.1135–54) in 1138 and proceeded to establish himself as the unrivalled political master of the region. As an expression of his power and wealth he founded religious institutions and castles across Yorkshire and Lincolnshire. These included the Augustinian house at Thornton, where he was buried, and his principal seat at Castle Bytham in Lincolnshire, where immense earthworks from the fortifications still survive.

Aumâle's work at Scarborough Castle, which probably began in the 1130s, was described later in the 12th century by the chronicler William of Newburgh. According to William, Aumâle was responsible for enclosing the headland with a wall and erecting a tower at the entrance, on the site of the present great tower.

But within a few years of its foundation Aumâle lost his new stronghold. When Henry II acceded to the throne in 1154 he demanded the return of all royal castles and Scarborough, which was actually built on a royal manor, was one of these. At first Aumâle defied the new king, but when Henry marched to York he reluctantly submitted and Scarborough Castle passed into the hands of the Crown.

A ROYAL CASTLE

In 1159 Henry II began to rebuild the castle at Scarborough, an operation that coincided with the development of the new town beneath its walls. His work to the castle is documented in the so-called Pipe Rolls, the accounts of the royal exchequer. About £650 was spent on the castle over the next ten years, an enormous sum of money at that time. The principal object of expenditure was the great tower, under construction from 1159 to 1169. William of Newburgh improbably claims that Henry built the new great tower because Aumâle's tower, probably little more than 20 years old, was decayed with age. Much more likely, the new great tower was intended to advertise unequivocally the fact that the castle had changed hands. Henry II also enclosed the great tower and its surrounding courtyard of domestic buildings with the inner bailey wall.

These changes proved to be a foretaste of yet more extensive alterations by King John between 1202 and 1212. He is known to have visited Scarborough several times and seems to have developed it, along with Knaresborough, as a major royal castle in Yorkshire. It is possible that he invested in Yorkshire to control the northern barons who opposed him. The Pipe Rolls show that he spent £2,291 on Scarborough during his reign – more than on any other individual castle in the kingdom. John's operations seem to have fallen into two distinct stages: first, the creation of an outer wall to the inner bailey between 1202 and 1206; and, second, the extension of that wall down to the cliff between 1207 and 1212. During the second stage he also constructed a hall in the inner bailey and the new royal chamber block with its separate great hall in the outer bailey. In 1215 the castle's well-supplied garrison comprised 10 knights, 72 sergeants and 13 crossbowmen.

John's son, Henry III (r.1216–72), was active in provisioning and maintaining the castle throughout his reign. Exposed as it was to the action of the sea and extreme weather, repair was an almost continuous and vastly expensive operation. A storm of 1237, for example, carried away the roofs of several castle buildings and in both 1241 and 1242 there were collapses of wall. Between 1243 and 1245, Henry also strengthened the barbican (the fortified entrance of the castle), rebuilding it with the present great bridge and a double drawbridge tower.

By the end of Henry III's reign Scarborough Castle was one of the greatest fortresses in England. Its importance is reflected by its nomination, along with the castles of Dover, Nottingham,

Above: This pottery fragment, shaped like a face, forms part of the decorative rim of a tall 13th-century Scarborough ware jug, used to serve drink
Below: A 13th-century depiction of the coronation of King John in 1199. He invested heavily in Scarborough and is thought to have built the curtain wall, the King's Hall and the chamber block

Bamburgh and Corfe, as a bargaining counter in the peace arrangements of 1265 between Henry III and his rebellious barons. After Henry III's death in 1272, Edward I (r.1272–1307) continued to use the castle as a royal lodging. In 1275 he held court and council at Scarborough and visited again in 1280. Prisoners from Edward's Scottish wars were also held here.

Piers Gaveston and the Siege of Scarborough Castle

When still Prince of Wales, the future Edward II (r.1307–27) became closely attached to Piers Gaveston, a young knight from Gascony in France. Gaveston was disliked by many of the nobility and was sent into exile in 1307 after a dramatic quarrel between Edward, Prince of Wales, and his father, Edward I. The prince had demanded that Gaveston be shown particular marks of favour and the king, furious at the request, drove him from the room, tearing out handfuls of his son's hair. When his father died, one of Edward's first acts was to recall Gaveston, who quickly became the object of bitter controversy between the new king and his barons. Edward's incompetence in government, combined with his infatuation, provoked the barons to demand that Gaveston be banished. In 1308 he was again sent into exile, but he returned the following year.

In 1312, after further confrontations, Edward went to the North of England with Gaveston to escape his opponents. His enemies acted quickly. Most of the royal household was captured in a surprise attack on Newcastle, from which Edward and Gaveston only just escaped. Gaveston then went on to Scarborough Castle, where he was besieged. A shortage of supplies forced him to surrender within a fortnight. He gave himself up after being promised safe conduct, but while he was being escorted back to the South an inveterate enemy, the Earl of Warwick, seized and summarily beheaded him.

Right: A 14th-century manuscript depiction of a castle under siege. Piers Gaveston, a favourite of the future Edward II, was besieged at Scarborough in 1312

Above: A reconstruction of the castle in about 1300. It shows the barbican **A** and its bridge **B** crossing the ditch. The great tower **C** sat within the inner bailey, which was entered through a gatehouse later known as the Constable Tower **D**. Along the line of the curtain wall is the chamber block **E** and the nearby King's Hall **F**. In the far distance is the chapel of Our Lady **G** on the site of the former Roman signal station

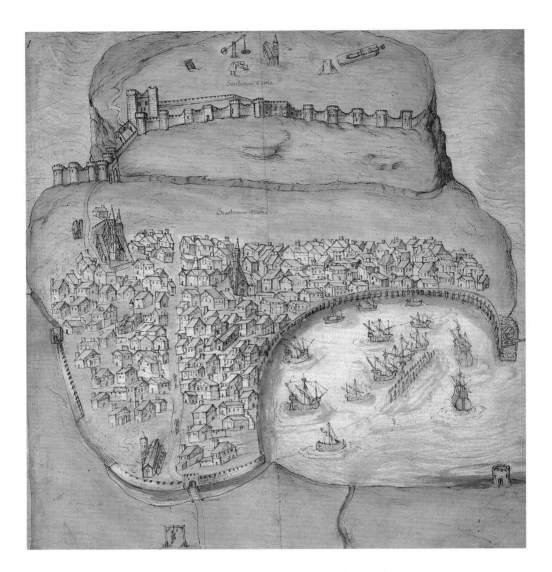

Above: An aerial view of Scarborough in 1538 made as part of a military survey of the coast. It shows the town and harbour beneath the castle on the headland. Visible in the town are two friary churches and the principal surviving town church

THE MEDIEVAL BOROUGH

Scarborough was a large medieval town that looked for its prosperity to the sea. It is laid out on an awkward site that slopes steeply across the promontory. Settlement has tended to concentrate near the harbour, which is first mentioned in a royal charter of 1253. In contrast, the upper town has remained lightly developed, leaving the parish church of St Mary isolated.

Henry II is credited with laying out 'old' and 'new' boroughs at Scarborough, both of which were defined by ditches and gates. The old borough was possibly established when he first seized the castle in 1155 and it may have subsumed an existing settlement. Henry II's regular grid of streets in the old borough is interrupted above the harbour at a natural break in the south cliff created by a stream called the Daymott. This break created easy access to the shore and was, therefore, an obvious position for a settlement. In the late Middle Ages, there existed at the same spot a church and market. Could these be the core of a pre-1155 settlement?

It is not clear why and at what date Henry II extended the town to the west by the addition of the new borough. Its street pattern is curiously disjointed from that of the old borough and comprises a series of curving streets that run up the slope. Whatever the case, it created a huge urban area by 12th-century standards, but there is no evidence that it ever had an especially large population.

THE LATE MEDIEVAL CASTLE

During the 14th and 15th centuries the castle seems to have undergone relatively little change. In 1308 Lord Percy – a baron who had inherited large interests in Yorkshire – and his wife were granted licence to reside in the castle and the family continued to live here intermittently for at least the next 40 years, undertaking minor repairs and building a bakehouse, brewhouse and kitchen in the inner bailey.

To judge from the evidence of occasional surveys of the fabric, the buildings were generally dilapidated and repaired only in extreme need. In this, Scarborough was typical of many royal castles. Kings rarely visited the castle and without this incentive to maintain the buildings, very little was done to them.

Unscrupulous constables and keepers probably added to the decay caused by age and the weather, removing valuable building materials and dressing up the loss as damage. The section of wall, for example, recorded by a clerk in 1361 as having collapsed and conveniently disappeared into a cloud of sand, sounds suspiciously as if it was quarried away.

The 14th century corresponded with the peak of the town's medieval prosperity. From about 1400 the town entered a gradual decline. The last king to visit the castle was Richard III (r.1483–5). In 1484 he stayed here while assembling a fleet to resist the expected invasion of Henry Tudor, later Henry VII.

THE CASTLE UNDER THE TUDORS

Even in its dilapidated state, Scarborough Castle continued to play an important role in times of crisis. During the 'Pilgrimage of Grace' in October 1536, a popular rebellion against Henry VIII's break with the Church of Rome, the constable, Sir Ralph Eure, declared his support for the king and was besieged in the castle. A truce struck on behalf of the king at York on 28 October brought hostilities in Scarborough to a brief halt, but shortly afterwards a ship loaded with supplies for the castle was seized by the rebels and the blockade resumed. The attack was clearly determined and a survey of the castle made in 1538 records damage done to it by gunfire. Nevertheless, the castle was held successfully against assault. Ralph's reward from the king included the guardianship of the castle for life.

Twenty years later the castle was again involved in a doomed plot against the Tudor monarchy. On 25 April 1557 Thomas Stafford, believing that he could incite a popular revolt

Above: A portrait of Richard III, the last monarch to stay at the castle. Richard established Scarborough as the centre of its own county and began work on new town fortifications. His early death in 1485 ended his plans
Below: A captain of the 'Pilgrimage of Grace', John Wyvill, was hanged in chains at Scarborough in 1537. This detail from the 1538 survey of the town may show his body hanging from the gallows outside the town gate

Right: In 1557 the castle was seized by Thomas Stafford in an unsuccessful bid to overthrow Queen Mary, shown here in 1554 in a portrait by Hans Eworth

Below: James I, painted by Paul van Somer in about 1620, united the thrones of England and Scotland. Scarborough was one of several royal castles he sold in what he thought of as the new heartland of his kingdom

against Queen Mary (r.1553–8), seized the castle and proclaimed himself Protector of the Realm. Some authorities claimed that he took the castle by stealth, others that he and his men simply wandered in and took control of the gates. The Earls of Shrewsbury and Westmorland retook the castle within six days, and Stafford was easily captured. Taken to London, he was tried and convicted for high treason, and was hanged and quartered at Tyburn on 28 May. His accomplices were executed at Scarborough and their bodies boiled and tanned for public exhibition. One result of the plot was that the governor of Scarborough was required to live in the castle to help guarantee its security. During the Northern Rising of 1569 – the attempt by some Catholic earls to unite the North in support of Mary Queen of Scots, who was being held prisoner in England – Elizabeth I (r.1558–1603) established a garrison at Scarborough. This was maintained until at least 1602.

THE ABANDONMENT OF SCARBOROUGH

The accession of James I in 1603 unified England and Scotland. Without fear of Scottish invasion several important northern castles were parcelled out into private hands. Scarborough was bought by a prominent local family, the Thompsons, and its land was rented as pasture; its days as a fortress seemed at an end. In the meantime, the town continued to decline: the corporation claimed in 1605 that 600 tenements lay empty.

THE CIVIL WAR

In September 1642, during the opening hostilities of the Civil War between Charles I (r.1625–49) and his Parliament, a local gentleman, Sir Hugh Cholmley, was sent with a commission to raise a regiment and hold Scarborough for Parliament. According to Cholmley's own vivid narrative of events, this force successfully occupied the town and the castle and was active in local skirmishes with Royalist forces for the next five months. But in that time Cholmley became disillusioned with Parliament and he was persuaded to change sides. Scarborough was an invaluable possession for the Royalist cause.

Charles I was dependent upon money, munitions and soldiers from the Continent, and his principal army in the North, at York, had no access to a harbour to allow the passage of supplies. Scarborough was therefore of great strategic importance in controlling coastal trade.

When Cholmley declared his backing for the king, his garrison consisted of 600 foot soldiers, 100 horsemen and 100 dragoons, or mounted soldiers. Those who chose to were allowed to leave, but not more than 20 did so. Immediately following this change of allegiance the castle was bloodlessly recaptured and then lost by Parliament. This happened while Cholmley was at York on a visit to Charles I. While he was away, 40 seamen, acting for Parliament and under the command of Cholmley's cousin Captain Browne Bushell, surprised the guard at night and took the castle. On hearing the news, Cholmley rushed back to Scarborough and successfully persuaded his relation to return the castle to him. For the next two years, between March 1643 and 1645, Scarborough served as an important Royalist base and its interception of shipping began to inflict serious coal shortages on London.

Above: 'When he [Cholmley] wanted money and could not borrow ... he made use of plate which was cut into pieces.' This piece of silver is a surviving example of this improvised currency. It is stamped with an image of Scarborough's great tower, the value of the counter in shillings and pence was calculated by its weight

Below: After the tower sheared in two an attempt was made to storm the castle. This reconstruction drawing shows the intense fighting that ensued over the ruins of the tower

Above: A 17th-century portrait of Lord Fairfax, a Parliamentarian general who visited Scarborough in 1644 and began negotiating the surrender of the castle
Below: Cannonballs found at the castle, probably dating from the time of the Civil War siege in 1645

The Siege of Scarborough

In 1644 the Royalist defeat at Marston Moor shattered the king's cause in the North and Parliamentary forces began to close in on the remaining Royalist strongholds in the area. Cholmley began to prepare for a siege at Scarborough, but his situation was not easy. He did not have the forces to defend the town and lacked adequate provisions. When the Parliamentarian general Lord Fairfax approached the town in August 1644, Cholmley entered into negotiations for surrender in order to buy himself time for preparation. His proposed terms – which included the demand that he appoint his own successor as governor of the castle – were outrageous, yet they were seriously considered by Parliament.

The extra time won by this ruse proved to be of critical importance when the siege, commanded by Fairfax's Lieutenant-General Sir John Meldrum, began. Sir Hugh was able to hold the town for three weeks before retreating into the castle on 18 February. Meldrum then tried to bully and cajole Cholmley into surrender but was eventually forced to bring up a siege train of guns, including one massive piece capable of firing a 64-pound ball. The church of St Mary below the castle was occupied by the Parliamentarians as one outpost, but to judge from the damage inflicted on the great tower the principal battery must have been on the rocky outcrop to the west of the castle. While setting up his guns there Meldrum toppled over the cliff trying to save his hat from the wind. Astonishingly, he survived the fall, but he was not on his feet again for six weeks.

When Meldrum recovered, the bombardment began. It was so intense that within three days the massive walls of the great tower split in two and half the building collapsed. An assault followed, but it was repulsed – the first of several close engagements in the early part of the siege. Meldrum was shot in the stomach and died shortly afterwards. The siege then changed character as the Parliamentary forces began to blockade the castle, which was now bombarded by both sea and land. In time, Cholmley ran out of gunpowder, then money

'The fall of the Tower was a very terrible spectacle, and more sudden than expected, at which the enemy gave a great shout, and the besieged, nothing dismayed, betook them to their arms, expecting an assault, by omission of which the enemy lost a fair opportunity, the falling part of the Tower having obstructed the passage to the gate house so that the guard there for present could have no release from their friends.'
Sir Hugh Cholmley, 1645

and finally food. Reduced by casualties and scurvy, at the end of five months there were only 25 soldiers fit for duty. Cholmley surrendered on 25 July 1645.

But this was not the end of Scarborough's service in the Civil War. Parliament ordered the repair of the castle and established a permanent garrison of 100 men, as well as 60 gunners for the batteries commanding the harbour. This force was put under the command of a trusted Parliamentarian, Colonel Boynton. But Parliament failed to pay the garrison and on 27 July 1648, when the Civil War flared up again, Boynton declared his loyalty to the imprisoned king by flying a red standard from the battlements. This time Parliament pressed home the siege of the castle and in December Boynton was forced to surrender. Instructions were now given that the castle be put beyond use – a process known as slighting – but opposition from the town preserved it from destruction.

Above: A portrait of Sir Hugh Cholmley, 1633, governor of Scarborough, who surrendered the castle in 1645
Below: A view of the castle by Francis Place, made in about 1700, showing the ruined tower and the roofs of buildings on the site of the master gunner's house

Below: Detail from a 19th-century portrait of George Fox by John Jewell Penstone. Fox, the founder of the Quakers, was imprisoned at Scarborough for his radical religious beliefs

'I had neither chimney nor firehearth. This being to the seaside and much open, the wind drove the rain in forcibly, so that the water came up over my bed and ran about the room that I was fain to skim it up with a platter.'
George Fox, 1666

THE REVIVAL OF SCARBOROUGH

Immediately after the Civil War, during continued hostilities with the Dutch, the castle, harbour batteries and garrison were kept in a state of defence. Nevertheless, in 1653 the Dutch Admiral De Witt sailed a small fleet into Scarborough bay and fired at a convoy of coal ships which were cowering against the shore under the protection of the batteries and nine men-of-war.

From the 1650s the castle served as a prison. Among those held here was George Fox, the founder of the Society of Friends, known as the Quakers. He was imprisoned several times for his radical religious beliefs and was held in the Cockhyll Tower at Scarborough between April 1665 and September 1666, the longest of any of his spells of imprisonment. He complained of the appalling conditions at Scarborough Castle. His cell was unheated and it flooded when it rained.

By 1688 the castle garrison had been run down and during the 'Glorious Revolution' – the sequence of events which led to James II's replacement on the throne by William of Orange and Mary (r.1689–1702) – Scarborough was seized by the Earl of Danby on behalf of the Protestant Prince of Orange. In the

Left: The Spa, *a plate from* The
Poetical Sketches of Scarborough,
*1813, by Papworth, Wrangham and
Combe. The picture is accompanied
by the following verse:*
'Tis now the busy crowd prepares
A visit to the Spa-Well stairs:
For Health like Truth, as sages tell,
Lies at the bottom of a well.'

event, the castle played no part in the overthrow of James II,
and nothing was immediately done to improve or repair
its defences.

Subsequent military surveys of the coast continue to
mention the castle, but it was not until the Jacobite rising of
1745 – the final, failed attempt to restore a Stuart to the
throne – that any significant measures were taken to restore
Scarborough. As a result of the rebellion, a barracks block was
constructed within the walls of King John's chamber block, and
this remained in use into the mid 19th century. Despite such
precautions, Scarborough remained vulnerable to attack and in
1779 the American commander and privateer John Paul Jones
engaged and defeated two men-of-war off Flamborough Head,
near Scarborough.

Scarborough as a Spa Town

From the 1660s Scarborough became famous as a fashionable
spa town, or 'Spaw' as it was called. It was the first English
seaside spa resort, where visitors could bathe in the sea, as
well as taking the waters. One description of 1660 talks of the
water bubbling up from the beach as if from a boiling pot. It
was said to have medicinal qualities that, according to its most

Above: Holidaymakers on
Scarborough Beach, c.1776,
by T. Ramsay. Scarborough
became a popular resort in
the 18th century

Below: Captain Charles Parker Catty
of the 46th Regiment, stationed at
Scarborough in 1855, posing with his
men on the great tower during a
recruiting exercise

enthusiastic advocates, offered relief from almost every
complaint. Great numbers of people flocked to the resort,
which flourished throughout the 18th century, and attracted
writers such as the diarist Celia Fiennes and Sarah, Duchess of
Marlborough. It also fostered the talents of an unusual host.
Dicky Dickinson, a disabled man, came to govern the social
protocol of the spa with an acerbic and earthy wit.

By the 1730s Scarborough became additionally associated
with an entirely new pastime: sea bathing for health and leisure.
Men were taken out into the water by boat and swam naked.
Women were decorously conveyed from the shore to the sea
in bathing machines that were drawn down the beach. It is a
reflection of how novel these practices were that a 1735
engraving of the town carefully detailed the swimming in the
middle distance.

It was not until the 1760s that the influx of visitors began to
transform the town. Up until this point, Scarborough had
continued to develop within its medieval bounds. Now elegant
terraces sprang up to accommodate visitors and the town
expanded rapidly. The arrival of the railway in 1845 opened up
Scarborough to mass tourism and also vastly increased the
population from 13,000 in 1851 to 33,000 in 1891. Scarborough
now became a prosperous holiday resort. The castle continued
to be garrisoned throughout this period; a Captain Charles
Parker Catty is known to have been stationed here in 1855.

The German Shelling

On the morning of 16 December 1914, in the opening months of the First World War, the sea fog around Scarborough lifted to reveal three German warships off the coast. One was laying mines in the distance, but two battle cruisers, the *Derrflinger* and *Von der Tann*, were in the bay itself and at 8.05am they opened fire on the town and castle. The castle wall and barracks were hit several times. The firing continued for 15 minutes and then, after a lull, the ships moved off at speed, firing again as they went. During this short attack, in which more than 500 shells were fired, 17 civilians were killed and more than 80 seriously wounded.

British public opinion was shocked that innocent civilians had been killed. On Friday 18 December 1914 the *Western Daily Press* reported one particularly tragic story:

'At a house in Wykeham Street, Scarborough, lived a family of six, named Bennett, and an old lady, an invalid; now only the father, one son and the old lady remain, and their residence is a ruin. The boy has given a pathetic account of his experiences. "I had just got out of bed", he said, "and was beginning to dress, when, what I should say was the fourth shot from the last, came crashing in. It hit the house fully, and fell through the bedroom into the kitchen. Everything fell on top of us all. Father and mother and two children were

GERMAN RAID DEC.16TH 1914. SHELLS EXPLODING ON THE CASTLE WALLS, SCARBOROUGH.

Above: This retouched photograph shows the bombardment of the castle and the destruction of the barracks

Below: A First World War enlistment poster, which used Scarborough as a rallying cry

downstairs in the kitchen. Father had called out to me, 'Come on, lad, let's away downstairs. It's the Germans. Come and look after mother.' But before I had time to get downstairs, it had all happened…. When at last I could look round me, I had only the shirt and a slipper on.

REMEMBER SCARBOROUGH!

ENLIST NOW

… I found mother and the children all up in one corner. … Mother was on a chair … she had lost her hand. … Father was covered with debris, but somehow he pulled himself out. I don't remember much about what happened after that, it was too terrible. My father and I got the others out as best we could. Eventually we moved mother into the yard, with little Jack and little George, but it was all too late. Mother was not dead when I was pulling them out, but she was gone by the time I got her into the yard. I then carried George into the next house, but he died as I put him down.'"

It is a mark of the outrage felt at the attack that 'Remember Scarborough!' became a rallying cry for recruiting officers across the nation. Three years later, on 4 September 1917, there was a second attack on Scarborough when a U-boat fired 30 shells at the town and minesweepers in the bay.

Above: The castle and great tower
against the unfailingly spectacular
backdrop of the sea and the North
Yorkshire coastline
Below: A photograph of the 1912
pageant, which was held in the castle

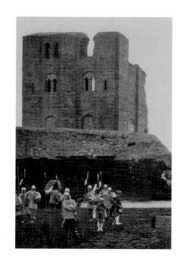

SCARBOROUGH FROM THE EARLY 20TH CENTURY TO THE PRESENT DAY

While Scarborough burgeoned as a tourist destination, ever more ambitious amusements were created for visitors. The famous Grand Hotel opened in 1867 and was the biggest hotel in Europe at the time. Shops and entertainment venues, including an aquarium and a pier, were also opened. In 1906 the town council leased the castle from the government with the intention of improving it as a visitor attraction. In 1912 it served as the setting for an extravagant historical pageant.

Just two years later in 1914, the castle and town were attacked by German warships at the beginning of the First World War. The castle wall and barracks block were badly damaged, as were parts of the town.

In 1920 Scarborough Castle was taken into state guardianship by the Ministry of Works. Under its ownership the 18th-century barracks block, damaged in the German bombardment, was demolished and the medieval fabric which it incorporated was exposed. The site of the Roman signal station and chapel was also excavated.

During the Second World War Scarborough suffered further damage, notably during a heavy air raid in March 1941. Its economy was slow to revive after the war and from the 1960s important Victorian buildings began, tragically, to disappear from the cityscape. Then, in 1981, the spa water was declared unfit for human consumption.

In recent years, however, the town has been enjoying something of a renaissance. Since 1984, the castle has been in the care of English Heritage, which continues to run it as a popular visitor attraction.

Contents

Introduction

I've been a quilter for more than 30 years and made hundreds of quilts, so it's become second nature for me to see quilt ideas everywhere I look. I'm constantly inspired to make quilts, but I also love making smaller items with fabric, such as totes, pouches, and sewing accessories. Because of my history as a quiltmaker, I often use traditional quilt blocks, motifs, and scraps as design elements in "non-quilt" objects.

If you're a quilter, chances are that you have orphan blocks from previous projects and have wondered what to do with them. Or perhaps you're looking for ways to extend your quilting skills into the world of three-dimensional sewing projects. I'm here to help! I've created and organized the designs in this book into pairs—one quilt and one non-quilt project, each featuring the same traditional motif.

You'll notice that I play around with the size and scale of quilt designs. It's natural to expect large projects to have large quilt blocks and small projects to include small blocks. Sometimes the projects in this book follow that process, but sometimes I switch things up and make small quilts with big blocks (or the other way around). Think outside the box (or the block) and have fun finding the perfect proportions for your project.

My hope in writing this book is that you'll see conventional quilt designs in a different way—that you'll find that these timeless, classic patterns can be used in more than just quilts. From there, maybe you'll be inspired to turn orphaned blocks into something useful, or look for ways to fashion your favorite quilt designs into something other than a quilt. You'll be surprised and delighted to discover where your quilting skills, and your imagination, can take you!

perfectly pretty
PATCHWORK
CLASSIC QUILTS, PILLOWS, PINCUSHIONS & MORE

Martingale®
Create with Confidence

Perfectly Pretty Patchwork:
Classic Quilts, Pillows, Pincushions & More
© 2019 by Kristyne Czepuryk

Martingale®
19021 120th Ave. NE, Ste. 102
Bothell, WA 98011-9511 USA
ShopMartingale.com

Printed in China
24 23 22 21 20 19   8 7 6 5 4 3 2 1

Library of Congress Cataloging-in-Publication Data is available upon request.

ISBN: 978-1-68356-025-8

MISSION STATEMENT

We empower makers who use fabric and yarn to make life more enjoyable.

CREDITS

PUBLISHER AND
CHIEF VISIONARY OFFICER
Jennifer Erbe Keltner

CONTENT DIRECTOR
Karen Costello Soltys

DESIGN MANAGER
Adrienne Smitke

MANAGING EDITOR
Tina Cook

PRODUCTION MANAGER
Regina Girard

ACQUISITIONS AND
DEVELOPMENT EDITOR
Laurie Baker

PHOTOGRAPHER
Brent Kane

TECHNICAL EDITOR
Ellen Pahl

ILLUSTRATOR
Sandy Loi

COPY EDITOR
Sheila Chapman Ryan

SPECIAL THANKS
Photography for this book was taken at the home of Lance and Jodi Allen of Snohomish, Washington.

DEDICATION

If seeing a quilt has ever inspired you to make something . . . anything . . . then this book is dedicated to you.

Irish Chain

Don't let your eye be fooled by this charming design. It's a simple combination
of alternating print squares and Nine Patch blocks. Can you see them?

Quilt

Finished quilt: 54½" × 60¾"
Finished block: 4½" × 4½"

The trick to making this quilt is matching the print
squares of each Nine Patch with the adjoining
unpieced setting squares, which differ on each
side. The time spent planning the layout and
fabric placement is well worth the striking finish.

MATERIALS

Yardage is based on 42"-wide fabric.

72 squares, 10" × 10", of assorted pink prints for
    blocks and setting triangles

1¾ yards of white print for blocks, setting triangles,
    and border

½ yard of pink print for binding

3½ yards of fabric for backing

61" × 67" piece of batting

CUTTING

From *each* of the assorted 10" squares, cut:
1 square, 5" × 5" (72 total)
4 squares, 2" × 2" (288 total)

From the white print, cut:
3 strips, 3⅜" × 42"; crosscut into 25 squares,
    3⅜" × 3⅜". Cut into quarters diagonally to
    make 100 triangles (2 are extra).
6 strips, 2" × 42"
16 strips, 2" × 42"; crosscut into 310 squares, 2" × 2"
2 squares, 2" × 2"; cut in half diagonally to make
    4 triangles

From the pink print, cut:
7 strips, 2" × 42"

BLOCKS AND SETTING TRIANGLES

Press seam allowances as indicated by the arrows in
the illustrations. The quilt must be planned and laid
out before sewing the Nine Patch blocks.

1 On a design wall or other flat surface, lay out the
pink 5" squares on point in nine horizontal rows

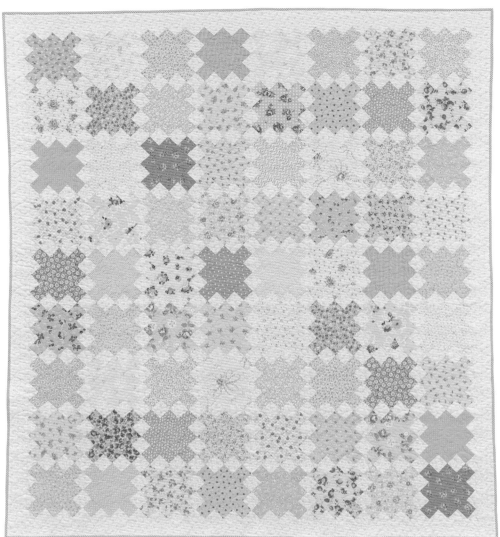

of eight squares each. Move them around until you're happy with the arrangement. You'll use this arrangement to make Nine Patch blocks for the interior of the quilt and pieced triangles to go around the sides.

2 Referring to the quilt assembly diagram on page 10 and beginning with the upper-left corner of your layout, select four print 2" squares that match the surrounding four print 5" squares. Arrange them together with five white 2" squares as shown at right to form a nine patch.

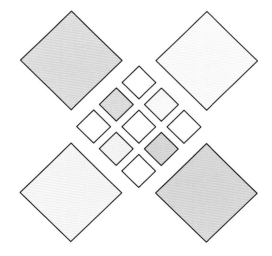

PERFECTLY PRETTY PATCHWORK

3 Make sure all of the pink squares are in the correct positions and then sew the squares into rows. Sew the rows together to make a Nine Patch block measuring 5" square, including seam allowances. Place the block in the correct empty space in the layout. Working across or down your layout, continue to make 56 blocks.

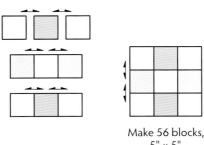

Make 56 blocks, 5" × 5".

4 Beginning along the top of the quilt layout, select two print 2" squares that match the two adjacent print 5" squares. Arrange them with one white 2" square and three white 3⅜" triangles. Make sure the pink squares are in the correct position, and then sew them together as shown. Place the side-setting triangle in the correct empty space in the layout. Working across the top and then clockwise around your layout, make 30 pieced side-setting triangles.

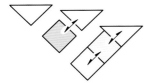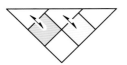

Make 30 units.

5 Beginning at the upper-left corner, select the print 2" square that matches the adjacent 5" square. Arrange and sew it together with two white 3⅜" triangles and one white 2" corner triangle as shown. Make a pieced triangle in the same manner for each corner.

Make 4 units.

ASSEMBLING THE QUILT

1 Sew the pink squares, Nine Patch blocks, and pieced side triangles into diagonal rows. Sew the rows together and add the pieced corner triangles. The quilt center should measure approximately 51½" × 57¾", including seam allowances.

2 Sew the white 2" × 42" strips together to make one long strip. Measure the length of the quilt through the center and cut two strips to that measurement. Sew the strips to the sides of the quilt. Measure the width of the quilt through the center, including the just-added borders, and cut two strips to that measurement. Sew the strips to the top and bottom. The quilt should measure approximately 54½" × 60¾".

FINISHING THE QUILT

Visit ShopMartingale.com/HowtoQuilt for help with any of the following finishing techniques.

1 Layer and baste your quilt, and quilt by hand or machine. The quilt shown is machine quilted in an overall design of flowers and leaves.

2 Using the pink 2" × 42" strips, prepare binding; attach the binding to the quilt.

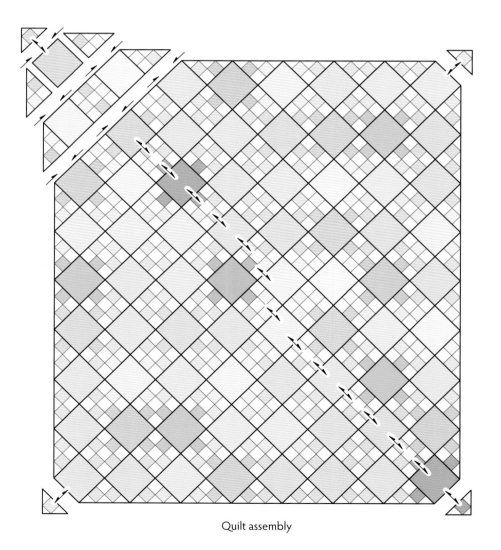

Quilt assembly

Pillow

Finished pillow: 17½" × 17½", excluding piping
Finished block: 1⅞" × 1⅞"

Making a coordinating pillow for a quilt is always a nice decorating detail. By simply reducing the scale of the blocks in a quilt, you can make an attractive room accessory. It's also a clever way to use scraps left over from the quilt (page 7).

MATERIALS

Yardage is based on 42"-wide fabric. Fat quarters measure 18" × 21".

25 squares, 5" × 5", of assorted pink prints for blocks and setting triangles

½ yard of white print for blocks, setting triangles, and border

1 fat quarter of pink print for piping

½ yard of fabric for backing

19" × 19" square of batting

2¼ yards of cording, ⅜" diameter

1 dress-weight zipper, at least 18" long

1 pillow form, 18" × 18"

Fabric basting spray (optional)

CUTTING

From *each* of the assorted print squares, cut:
1 square, 2⅜" × 2⅜" (25 total)
4 squares, 1⅛" × 1⅛" (100 total)

From the white print, cut:
2 strips, 3" × 42"
1 strip, 2⅛" × 42"; crosscut into:
    14 squares, 2⅛" × 2⅛"; cut into quarters
      diagonally to make 56 triangles
    2 squares, 1½" × 1½"; cut in half diagonally
      to make 4 triangles
3 strips, 1⅛" × 42"; crosscut into 96 squares,
    1⅛" × 1⅛"

From the pink print, cut:
1¾"-wide bias strips to total 80"
1 rectangle, 2" × 2½"

From the backing fabric, cut:
1 rectangle, 15½" × 18"
1 rectangle, 6½" × 18"

MAKING THE BLOCKS AND SETTING TRIANGLES

Press seam allowances as indicated by the arrows in the illustrations or as otherwise stated. The pillow top must be planned and laid out before sewing the Nine Patch blocks.

1 On a design wall or other flat surface, lay out the pink 2⅜" squares on point in five horizontal rows of five squares each. Move them around until you're happy with the arrangement. You'll use this arrangement to make Nine Patch blocks for the interior and pieced triangles to go around the sides.

2 Referring to the pillow assembly diagram on page 13 and beginning with the upper-left corner of your layout, select four print 1⅛" squares that match the surrounding four print squares. Arrange them together with five white 1⅛" squares as shown on page 13. Make sure the pink squares are in the correct positions and then sew the squares into

PERFECTLY PRETTY PATCHWORK

rows. Sew the rows together to make the Nine Patch block. Place the block in the correct empty space in the layout. The block should measure 2⅜" square, including seam allowances. Working across or down your layout, continue to make 16 blocks.

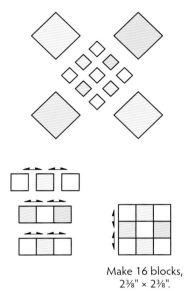

Make 16 blocks,
2⅜" × 2⅜".

3 Beginning along the top of the pillow layout, select two print 1⅛" squares that match the two adjacent print 2⅜" squares. Arrange them together with one white 1⅛" square and three white 2⅛" triangles. Make sure the pink squares are in the correct position, and then sew them together as shown. Place the side-setting triangle in the correct empty space in the layout. Working across the top and then clockwise around your layout, make 16 pieced side-setting triangles.

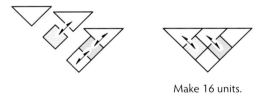

Make 16 units.

4 Beginning at the upper-left corner, select the print 1⅛" square that matches the adjacent 2⅜" square. Arrange and sew it together with two white 2⅛" triangles and one white corner 1½" triangle as

shown. Make a pieced triangle in the same manner for each corner.

Make 4 units.

ASSEMBLING THE PILLOW TOP

1 Sew the pink squares, Nine Patch blocks, and pieced side triangles into diagonal rows. Sew the rows together and add the pieced corner triangles. The pillow top should measure approximately 13¾" square, including seam allowances.

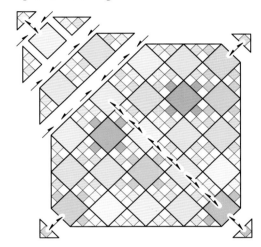

Pillow assembly

2 Measure the pillow top through the center and cut two strips to that measurement from the white 3" × 42" strips. Sew the strips to the sides of the pillow top. Measure the width of the top, including the just-added borders, and cut two strips to that measurement. Sew the strips to the top and bottom. The pillow top should measure approximately 18¾" × 18¾".

3 Layer and baste the pillow top with the batting, and quilt by hand or machine. I machine quilted an allover floral design. You can add a 19" square of muslin or other light fabric to the other side of the batting if you like, or quilt just the two layers.

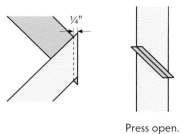

2 Sew the bias strips together with diagonal seams to make a strip approximately 80" long.

Press open.

3 Lay the cording along the wrong side of the bias strip. Fold the fabric strip in half, wrong sides together, and pin the edges closed. Using a zipper foot on your sewing machine, sew the bias strips next to the cording to make the piping. Trim excess cording at the ends.

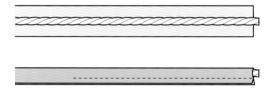

4 Trim the pillow top to measure 18" square, keeping the borders even all around. Trim the batting from the seam allowances to reduce bulk.

MAKING AND ADDING THE PIPING

1 To make a tab for covering the raw edges of the piping, fold the pink 2" × 2½" rectangle along the 2½" length approximately in thirds with the raw edge positioned in the middle. Press the folds.

Make 1 tab, 1" × 2½".

4 Lay the tab made in step 1 on the pillow front in the center of the bottom edge, aligning raw edges. Baste in place. Lay one end of the piping in the center of the tab, aligning the raw edges of the piping with the raw edges of the pillow. Pin the piping in place around the pillow, rounding it gently at the corners. Using a zipper foot, sew the piping in place. Trim excess piping where the ends meet.

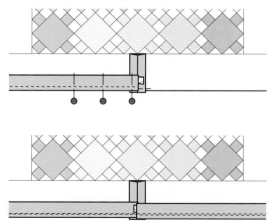

5 Fold the remaining edge of the tab over the ends of the piping and sew it in place. Trim the excess tab fabric.

6 Trim the corners of the pillow top to match the piping and reduce bulk.

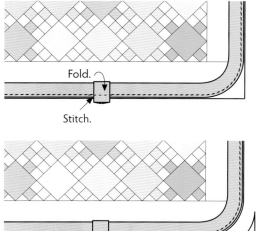

Fold. Stitch.

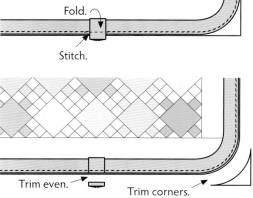

Trim even. Trim corners.

MAKING THE ZIPPERED BACK

1 Fold one 18" edge of the 15½" × 18" backing rectangle over 1" twice. Sew ⅛" from the inner folded edge to make a hem.

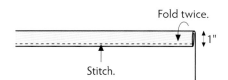

Fold twice. 1" Stitch.

2 Place the zipper along the edge of the 6½" × 18" backing rectangle, right sides together and with the zipper edge aligned with the raw edge of the fabric. Using a zipper foot, sew the zipper using a ¼" seam allowance. Press the fabric away from the zipper.

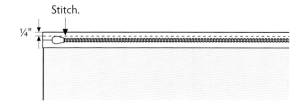

Stitch. ¼"

3 Place the hemmed edge of the backing rectangle over the zipper so that it overlaps and covers the zipper. Pin and sew the zipper in place using a zipper foot.

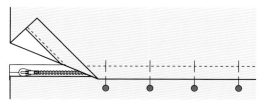

Cover zipper and stitch.

4 Baste the layers together at both ends of the zipper using a scant ¼" seam allowance.

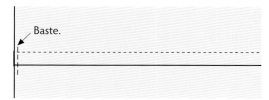

Baste.

ASSEMBLING THE PILLOW

1 Lay the pillow front and back right sides together. Trim the backing to the same size as the front and open the zipper halfway.

2 Pin the back to the front, and with the zipper foot attached to the machine, sew them together, stitching along the same stitching line as the piping. Turn the pillow cover right side out through the zipper opening and insert the pillow form.

Zipper Fitting

If you're working with a zipper that's too long, position it so that the zipper pull end is extending beyond the pillow back. After sewing the zipper in place, open the zipper halfway and trim away the excess from the top end. Just make sure to stitch that end of the zipper closed before zipping up the zipper!

Honeybee

Bee wings—embroidered on the mini-quilt and appliquéd on the tote bag—elevate the otherwise utilitarian Nine Patch block to new design heights.

Mini-Quilt

Finished quilt: 11¾" × 11¾"
Finished block: 1⅞" × 1⅞"

This charming mini-quilt features tiny embroidered honeybee details that are typically appliquéd on a larger quilt block. The Nine Patch blocks, are the perfect home for tiny bits of leftover fabrics.

MATERIALS

Fat quarters measure 18" × 21"; fat eighths measure 9" × 21".

36 scraps, at least 1¼" × 1¼", of assorted yellow prints for blocks

1 fat eighth of white print for sashing

1 fat quarter of pink solid for inner border and backing

1 fat quarter of yellow stripe for outer border

1 fat eighth of pink print for binding

16" × 16" piece of batting

1 skein pink embroidery floss

FriXion pen or other removable fabric marker

Fabric basting spray (optional)

CUTTING

From *each* yellow scrap, cut:
1 square, 1⅛" × 1⅛" (36 total)

From the white print, cut:
2 strips, 1½" × 21"; crosscut into:
    2 rectangles, 1½" × 7¼"
    3 rectangles, 1½" × 5¼"
    2 rectangles, 1½" × 2⅜"

From the pink solid, cut:*
2 strips, 1" × 18"; crosscut into:
    2 strips, 1" × 8¼"
    2 strips, 1" × 7¼"

From the yellow stripe, cut:
4 strips, 2¼" × 16"

From the pink print, cut:
3 strips, 2" × 21"

*Cut the strips along the 18" length for most efficient use of your fabric. Reserve the remaining fabric for backing.

to the top and bottom. The quilt center should measure 7¼" square, including seam allowances.

3 Sew pink 1" × 7¼" strips to the sides of the quilt and then add the pink 1" × 8¼" strips to the top and bottom. The quilt center should measure 8¼" square, including seam allowances.

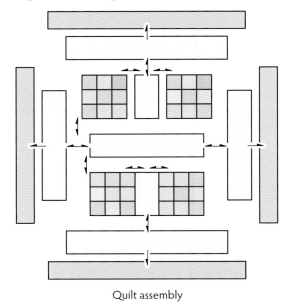

Quilt assembly

4 Using the embroidery pattern on pattern sheet 1, trace the honeybee wings onto the white fabric at the block corners with the fabric marker. Embroider the wings with a stem stitch using one strand of floss. Using two strands of floss, stitch colonial knots (or French knots) at the corners of all the squares. Refer to "Embroidery Basics" on page 78 for stitching details.

MAKING THE BLOCKS

Join nine assorted yellow 1⅛" squares to form a Nine Patch block, pressing seam allowances open. The block should measure 2⅜" square, including seam allowances. Make four blocks.

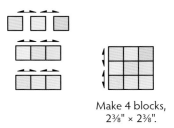

Make 4 blocks,
2⅜" × 2⅜".

ASSEMBLING THE QUILT CENTER

Press seam allowances as indicated by the arrows in the illustrations.

1 Arrange the blocks in two rows of two blocks each. Place a white 1½" × 2⅜" rectangle between the blocks in each row and a white 1½" × 5¼" rectangle between the rows. Sew the blocks and sashing into rows, and then sew the rows together.

2 Sew two white 1½" × 5¼" rectangles to the sides of the quilt. Add the white 1½" × 7¼" rectangles

Not Your Typical Knot

I'm a big fan of colonial knots. I prefer them to French knots; I find them easier to stitch and less likely to become tangled. The result is nice and flat, like a doughnut, rather than a twisted nub. The time it takes to learn this knot is well worth it both in terms of avoiding tangled threads and in the look of the finished knot.

PERFECTLY PRETTY PATCHWORK

ADDING THE MITERED BORDER

1 Center and pin a yellow 2¼" × 16" strip to one side of the quilt. If you're using a stripe, adjust the position of the strips in order to match the stripes at each corner. Sew the border to the quilt, starting and stopping ¼" from each end. Sew a few reinforcing stitches at both ends of the seam. Repeat with the remaining three sides.

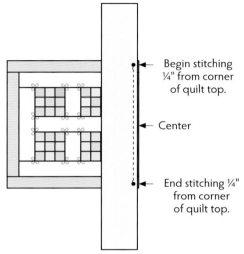

Begin stitching ¼" from corner of quilt top.

Center

End stitching ¼" from corner of quilt top.

2 Fold the quilt top diagonally at the corner so the adjoining borders are flat with right sides together. Use a fabric marker and a ruler with a 45° line to mark a seam starting at the reinforcing stitches. Pin and sew the borders together. Trim the seam allowances to ¼".

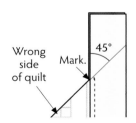

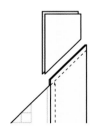

Wrong side of quilt

Mark.

45°

3 Repeat with each of the remaining corners to complete the quilt top and press. The quilt top should measure 11¾" square.

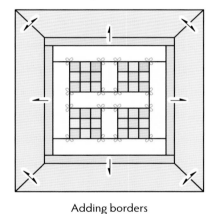

Adding borders

FINISHING THE QUILT

Visit ShopMartingale.com/HowtoQuilt for help with any of the following finishing techniques.

1 Layer and baste your quilt, and quilt as desired. The quilt shown is hand quilted, outlining the blocks and border seams.

2 Using the pink 2" × 21" strips, prepare binding; attach the binding to the quilt.

PERFECTLY PRETTY PATCHWORK

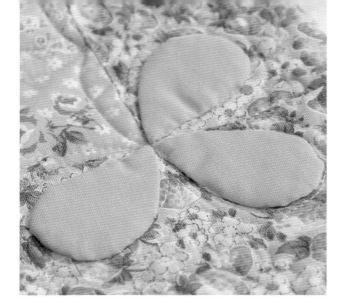

Tote Bag

Finished tote: 11" × 14½"
Finished block: 6" × 6"

Sometimes all a quilter needs in order to design a handsome tote bag is a single quilt block. Whether it's a test block that turned out well, an extra block that resulted from a miscount, or a favorite block made for fun, here's the perfect pattern for an orphan block.

MATERIALS

Yardage is based on 42"-wide fabric. Fat eighths measure 9" × 21".

9 squares, 2½" × 2½", of assorted yellow prints for Nine Patch block

½ yard of yellow floral for bag and handle units

1 fat eighth of yellow solid for wing appliqués

½ yard of fabric for lining

1 yard of handle webbing, 1½" wide

1 square, 2" × 2", of fabric for decorative tab

2" length of double-edged lace, ⅝" to ¾" wide, for tab

12" × 30" piece of batting

Template plastic or freezer paper

Fabric basting spray (optional)

CUTTING

Using the pattern on page 24, make a template for the wing.

From the yellow floral, cut:
1 rectangle, 11½" × 21"
1 rectangle, 3" × 11½"
2 rectangles, 2" × 10½"
2 rectangles, 3" × 6½"

From the yellow solid, cut:
12 wings using the template; add a ¼" seam allowance for turned-edge appliqué

From the lining fabric, cut:
1 rectangle, 11½" × 29½"

From the handle webbing, cut:*
2 lengths, 1½" × 15"

*Cut the 1-yard length of webbing in half if you'd like the handles to be longer.

MAKING THE BAG BODY

Press seam allowances as indicated by the arrows in the illustrations or as otherwise stated.

1 Sew the nine assorted yellow 2½" squares together to form a Nine Patch block, pressing seam allowances open. The block should measure 6½" square, including seam allowances.

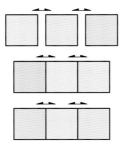 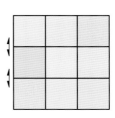

Make 1 block,
6½" × 6½".

2 Sew the floral 3" × 6½" rectangles to the sides of the block. Sew the 3" × 11½" rectangle to the top and the 11½" × 21" rectangle to the bottom.

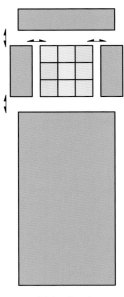

Make 1 unit,
11½" × 29½".

3 Prepare 12 wings for your preferred appliqué method. Position and appliqué three bee wings to each corner of the Nine Patch block, referring to the photograph on page 20 for placement. Visit ShopMartingale.com/HowtoQuilt for free, downloadable instructions if you need appliqué help.

Dark Shadows

If the fabric underneath the wing appliqués shows through, cut away the background fabric behind each. Maintain a ¼" seam allowance, and avoid cutting the appliqué fabric.

4 Layer the tote exterior with the batting rectangle. Pin or spray baste the two layers together and quilt by hand or machine. I quilted arcs in the squares and an overall floral pattern in the background. Trim the batting even with the tote exterior edges.

MAKING THE TAB

1 Fold the 2" × 2" square of fabric for the tab in half, right sides together, and sew along the 2" sides using a ¼" seam allowance. Turn the tube right side out and press with the seam centered on one side.

Fold

Center seam
and press.

2 Hand or machine sew the 2" length of lace to the right side of the fabric tab. Fold the tab in half, wrong sides together, and baste the raw edges together with a scant ¼" seam.

Baste.

Fold.

3 Pin and baste the tab to the left edge of the bag exterior, 11" from the top edge.

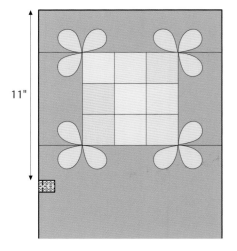

11"

4 Fold the tote exterior in half, right sides together, and sew both sides. Turn the bag right side out.

MAKING THE HANDLES

1 To make a handle unit, fold a floral 2" × 10½" rectangle in half, right sides together, and sew the short edges together. Press seam allowances open and center the seam allowance along one side. Then sew one of the long edges together. Turn right side out. The handle unit should measure 1¾" × 5". Make two.

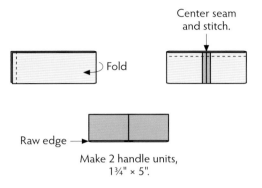

Center seam and stitch.

Fold

Raw edge →

Make 2 handle units,
1¾" × 5".

2 Find the center of a webbing strip. Fold the edges of the handle over in the middle 5" as shown. Pin into position. Wrap this 5" section with a handle unit from the previous step, overlapping the raw edge with the sewn edge. Hand sew the long edges together and sew the short edges to the handle webbing. Repeat with the other handle.

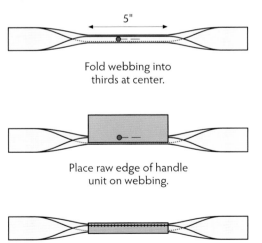

5"

Fold webbing into thirds at center.

Place raw edge of handle unit on webbing.

Wrap handle unit around webbing.
Cover raw edge with sewn edge and stitch.

3 Find the center of the bag front along the top. Pin the handles to the top of the tote, aligning the raw edges. Space the inside edges of the handles 4" apart and 2" from the middle as shown. Baste them in place with a scant ¼" seam allowance. Repeat with the other handle on the bag back.

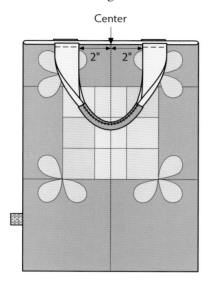

ASSEMBLING THE TOTE

1 Fold the lining rectangle in half, right sides together, and sew both sides. Leave a 5" opening along one side seam.

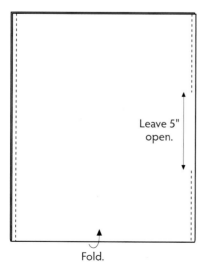

Leave 5" open.

Fold.

2 With the tote right side out and the lining inside out, insert the tote into the lining. Pin and sew the pieces together around the top edge. Turn the tote right side out through the opening in the lining and sew the opening closed by hand or machine.

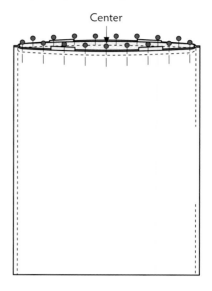

Center

3 Insert the lining inside the tote and press all the seams flat to shape the tote.

Pattern does not include seam allowance.

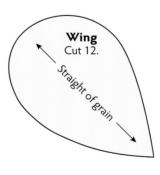

Wing
Cut 12.

Straight of grain

Mill and Stars

The playful Mill and Stars block looks beautiful in just about any color and value combination you can imagine. Instead of a light fabric for the background, consider a dark background with light prints for the stars. Or use many low-volume prints for a scrappy but homogeneous background.

Quilt

Finished quilt: 66½" × 66½"
Finished blocks: 3" × 3" and 6" × 6"

Varying the block size in a quilt adds interest and personality. Here, 6" blocks frame a center medallion of 3" blocks. I think it would be fun—and the quilt would take on a very different look—if the blocks were reversed, with a single large block in the center surrounded by a field of smaller blocks.

MATERIALS

Yardage is based on 42"-wide fabric.

28 squares, 10" × 10", of assorted green prints for blocks

28 squares, 10" × 10", of assorted blue prints for blocks

5⅓ yards of white solid for blocks and borders

¼ yard of green solid for inner border

½ yard of blue print for binding

4⅛ yards of fabric for backing

73" × 73" piece of batting

Template plastic

CUTTING

Using the patterns on pattern sheet 1, make templates A–D for the kites and triangles.

From *each* assorted blue print, cut:
6 kites using template A (168 total)
2 kites using template C (56 total; 6 are extra)

From *each* assorted green print, cut:
6 kites using template A (168 total)
2 kites using template C (56 total; 6 are extra)

From the white solid, cut *on the lengthwise grain*:
4 strips, 3½" × 70"

Continued on page 27

Continued from page 25

From the *remainder* of the white solid, cut:

336 triangles using template B

336 triangles using template B reversed

100 triangles using template D

100 triangles using template D reversed

4 strips, 2½" × 42"; crosscut into:

    2 strips, 2½" × 24½"

    2 strips, 2½" × 20½"

2 strips, 1½" × 42"; crosscut into:

    2 strips, 1½" × 17½"

    2 strips, 1½" × 15½"

From the green solid, cut:

2 strips, 2" × 42"; crosscut into:

    2 strips, 2" × 20½"

    2 strips, 2" × 17½"

From the blue print, cut:

7 strips, 2" × 42"

MAKING THE BLOCKS

Press seam allowances as indicated by the arrows in the illustrations or as otherwise stated.

1 To make the 6½" blocks, sew a white B triangle and a B reversed triangle to a green or blue A kite shape. Make a total of 336 pieced triangles and keep them organized in matching pairs. There should be 168 pairs, 84 blue and 84 green.

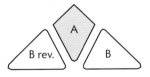

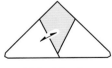

Make 84 pairs.

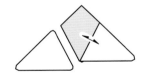

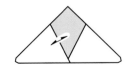

Make 84 pairs.

2 Choose a matching pair of green triangles and a matching pair of blue triangles. Sew one of each pair together as shown to make two half blocks. Sew the half blocks together. The block should measure 6½" square, including seam allowances. Make 84 blocks.

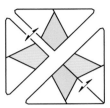

Make 84 blocks, 6½" × 6½".

3 Repeat step 1 with the green and blue C kite shapes and white D and D reversed triangles. Make 100 pieced triangles and keep them organized in matching pairs, 25 blue and 25 green.

Make 25 pairs.   Make 25 pairs.

4 Repeat step 2 to make a block measuring 3½" square, including seam allowances. Make 25 blocks.

Make 25 blocks, 3½" × 3½".

ASSEMBLING THE QUILT CENTER

In the quilt shown, the blue shapes are oriented horizontally and the green shapes are vertical. Decide if you want your quilt to have intentional or random color placement. (Both ways are pretty!)

1 Referring to the quilt center assembly diagram on page 28, arrange and sew the 3½" blocks into five rows of five blocks each. Sew the rows together. The quilt center should measure 15½" square, including seam allowances.

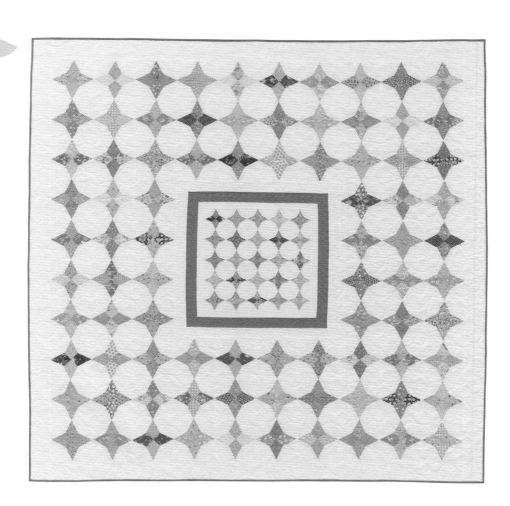

2 Sew the white 1½" × 15½" strips to the sides of the quilt center. Sew the white 1½" × 17½" strips to the top and bottom.

3 Sew the green solid 2" × 17½" strips to the sides and the 2" × 20½" strips to the top and bottom.

4 Sew the white 2½" × 20½" strips to the sides and the 2½" × 24½" strips to the top and bottom as shown at right. The quilt center should measure 24½" square, including seam allowances.

ASSEMBLING THE QUILT

1 Referring to the assembly diagram on page 29, arrange and sew 30 of the 6½" blocks together into three rows of 10 blocks each to make the bottom section of the quilt. Press seam allowances open. Repeat to make another section for the quilt top.

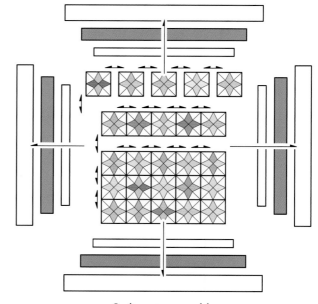

Quilt center assembly

PERFECTLY PRETTY PATCHWORK

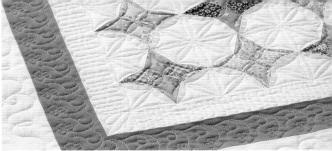

2 Sew 12 of the 6½" blocks together into four rows of three blocks each to make a side section. Press seam allowances open. Make two side sections.

3 Sew the side sections to the quilt center. Then sew the top and bottom sections to the top and bottom to complete the quilt interior. It should measure 60½" square, including seam allowances.

4 Cut the white 3½" × 70" strips into two strips 60½" long and two strips 66½" long. Sew the 60½" strips to the sides of the quilt and the 66½" strips to the top and bottom. The quilt top should measure 66½" square.

FINISHING THE QUILT

Visit ShopMartingale.com/HowtoQuilt for help with any of the following finishing techniques.

1 Layer and baste your quilt, and quilt by hand or machine. The quilt shown is machine quilted with a sand-dollar design that follows the seams between the stars in the medallion center. The first white border is quilted with a short switchback design, the inner green border is quilted with a repeated floral design, and the balance of the quilt features an allover design of swirls and flowers.

2 Using the blue 2" × 42" strips, prepare binding; attach the binding to the quilt.

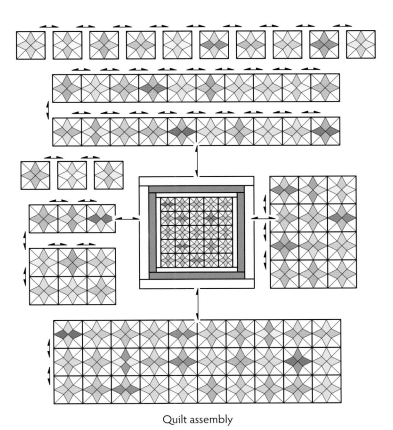

Quilt assembly

PERFECTLY PRETTY PATCHWORK

Pincushions

Finished pincushions

❋ 3" × 3" × 1½",
❋ 4" × 4" × 1½",
❋ 5" × 5" × 1½"

Almost any leftover quilt block can be turned into a pincushion. Here are three handy little cushions made in graduating sizes. I'm sure at least one will suit your needs. You may want to assign each pincushion to hold a different type of needle—sharps, appliqué, betweens, embroidery—oops, looks like we need a fourth pincushion!

MATERIALS FOR 1 PINCUSHION (ANY SIZE)

1 scrap, 4" × 5", of blue print for block

1 scrap, 4" × 5", of green print for block

1 scrap, 7" × 9", of light print for block

1 strip, 2" × 22", of print fabric for sides

1 square, 6" × 6", of fabric for bottom

2 squares, 6" × 6", of batting

2" × 22" strip of fusible interfacing (optional)*

Template material: plastic, freezer paper, or other paper

Ground walnut shells for filling

Funnel for adding filling

1 shank button

1 two-hole button

Button thread or quilting thread

3" or 4" doll needle

Fabric basting spray (optional)

Interfacing will minimize the release of dust from the walnut shells. It also helps to prevent the dark color of the shells from showing through light-colored fabrics.

CUTTING

Template patterns are on pattern page 1.

For the 3" Pincushion

Use the C and D patterns to make templates.

From *each* of the green and blue scraps, cut:
2 kites using template C (4 total)

From the light print, cut:
4 triangles using template D
4 triangles using template D reversed

From the print strip for sides, cut:
1 strip, 2" × 12½"

From the interfacing, cut:
1 strip, 1½" × 12"

For the 4" Pincushion

Use the E and F patterns to make templates.

From *each* of the green and blue scraps, cut:
2 kites using template E (4 total)

From the light print, cut:
4 triangles using template F
4 triangles using template F reversed

From the print strip for sides, cut:
1 strip, 2" × 16½"

From the interfacing, cut:
1 strip, 1½" × 16"

For the 5" Pincushion

Use the G and H patterns to make templates.

From *each* of the green and blue scraps, cut:
2 kites using template G (4 total)

From the light print, cut:
4 triangles using template H
4 triangles using template H reversed

From the print strip for sides, cut:
1 strip, 2" × 20½"

From the interfacing, cut:
1 strip, 1½" × 20"

MAKING THE BLOCK

Instructions are for one pincushion of any size. Press seam allowances as indicated by the arrows in the illustrations or as otherwise stated.

1 Sew a light triangle and a light triangle reversed to a green or blue kite shape. Make two green units and two blue units.

2 Sew the pieced units together in pairs to make two half blocks. Sew the half blocks together. The block should measure 3½" square, 4½" square, or 5½" square, including seam allowances—depending on the block size you're making.

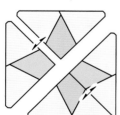 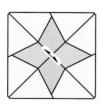

Make 1 block.

ASSEMBLING THE PINCUSHION

1 Pin or spray baste a batting square to the wrong side of the block and quilt as desired. I hand quilted ⅛" inside every patchwork shape. Repeat with the bottom square and batting. I quilted the bottom with ½" crosshatching. Trim the batting to the same size as the block; repeat for the bottom square.

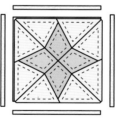

Trim batting even.   Trim backing to same size as front.

2 Center and fuse the interfacing strip on the wrong side of the 2"-wide strip for the sides, following the manufacturer's instructions. Fold the strip in half, right sides together, and sew the short edges together. Sew a few reinforcing stitches on both ends of this seam and press open.

Stitch.

3 Fold and mark the center of the side strip with a pin. Pin the side to the block, right sides together, matching the pin to a star point on the block. Pin the opposite side, matching the seam to the opposite star point. Continue to pin each side.

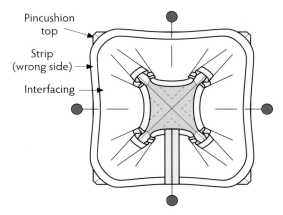

Pincushion top

Strip (wrong side)

Interfacing

4 Sew the strip to one side of the block, starting and stopping ¼" away from each corner and sewing a few backstitches at each end. Clip the seam allowance at the corner as shown. Repeat this process for all four sides.

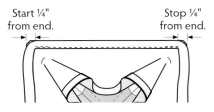

Start ¼" from end.   Stop ¼" from end.

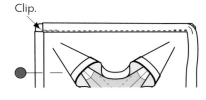

Clip.

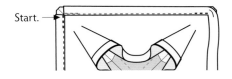

Start.

5 Fold the sides at each corner, right sides together, and mark the folds with a pin. Then pin and sew the bottom square to the sides in the same manner as for the top, aligning the corners of the bottom square with the pins and leaving a 2" opening along one edge.

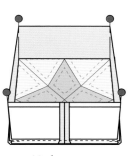
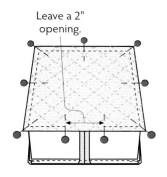

Leave a 2" opening.

Mark corners.

6 Trim the excess bulk in the seam allowances at the corners, and turn the pincushion right side out.

7 Using the funnel, fill the pincushion with ground walnut shells. Pin and stitch the opening closed.

8 Using the doll needle and button thread, sew the shank button to the top and the two-hole button to the pincushion bottom, centering them both. Pull the thread tight from top to bottom and go back and forth several times. To end, wrap the thread around the bottom button a few times. Then insert the needle and bring it out close to the seam along the bottom. Knot the thread and insert the needle back through the same hole and out an inch or so away. Gently tug to pull the knot into the seam to hide it. Trim the thread end.

Checkerboard

The checkerboard is arguably the most traditional patchwork design. It's iconic. It's elegantly simple. And it's oh-so versatile. Both projects in this pairing feature checkerboard patchwork set on point, which adds interest to the designs.

Quilt

Finished quilt: 71⅝" × 71⅝"
Finished block: 10⅝" × 10⅝"

I think most non-quilters conjure up some sort of checkerboard image in their head when they hear the word *quilt*. I designed this project to look like a vintage heirloom, made by someone who used precious and favorite scraps from his or her basket, mostly pairing light and dark prints, but occasionally making do with what was available.

MATERIALS

Yardage is based on 42"-wide fabric.

25 squares, 12" × 12", of assorted dark prints for blocks*

25 squares, 10" × 10", of assorted light prints for blocks*

1½ yards of pink solid for sashing and sashing squares

3 yards of white solid for blocks and sashing

⅝ yard of pink print for binding

4⅓ yards of fabric for backing

78" × 78" piece of batting

The 12" squares are cut to create the block squares that are positioned along the block's outer edges; the 10" squares are cut to create the squares positioned in the block interior. For simplicity they are designated "darks" and "lights," but the values can be swapped as long as there's contrast between the two fabrics in each block. You'll notice some blocks are made of two mediums in contrasting colors.

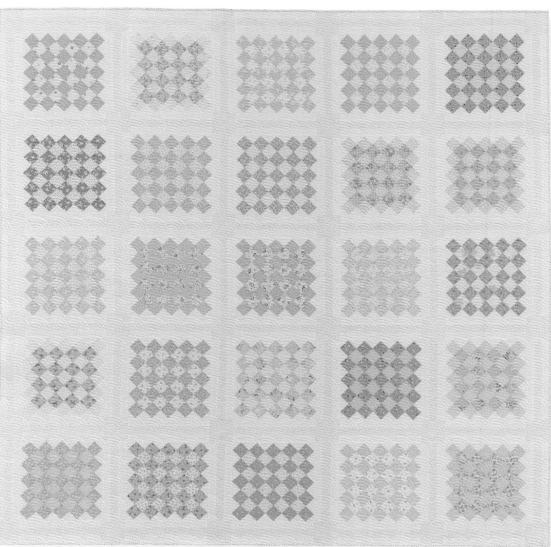

CUTTING

Keep like prints and sizes together when cutting.

From *each* of the assorted dark prints, cut:
25 squares, 2" × 2" (625 total)

From *each* of the assorted light prints, cut:
16 squares, 2" × 2" (400 total)

From the pink solid, cut:*
3 strips, 11⅛" × 42"; crosscut into 60 strips,
    1½" × 11⅛"
4 strips, 3½" × 42"; crosscut into 36 squares,
    3½" × 3½"

From the white solid, cut:*
5 strips, 11⅛" × 42"; crosscut into 120 strips,
    1½" × 11⅛"
10 strips, 3½" × 42"; crosscut into 100 squares,
    3½" × 3½". Cut into quarters diagonally to make
    400 triangles.
3 strips, 2" × 42"; crosscut into 50 squares, 2" × 2".
    Cut in half diagonally to make 100 triangles.

From the pink print, cut:
8 strips, 2" × 42"

**See "Before You Cut" on page 37 before cutting
the pink and white solids.*

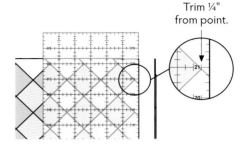

Before You Cut

Each block has 61 pieces. When sewing together this many pieces, a tiny variance in cutting or seam allowances can affect precision. Consider making a few blocks before cutting the strips for the sashing to double-check your measurements. If you find you can't trim the blocks to measure exactly 11⅛" square, trim them all to a consistent size, making sure to leave the ¼" seam allowance beyond the points of the squares. Then cut the sashing strips to match the blocks. This will ensure a perfect finish.

MAKING THE BLOCKS

Press seam allowances as indicated by the arrows in the illustrations or as otherwise stated. The instructions are written to make one block at a time.

For each block, you'll need:

* 1 set of 25 dark 2" squares

* 1 set of 16 light 2" squares

* 16 white 3½" triangles

* 4 white 2" triangles

1 Arrange and sew the dark and light squares and white 3½" side triangles on point in nine diagonal rows. Join the rows. Add the white 2" corner triangles.

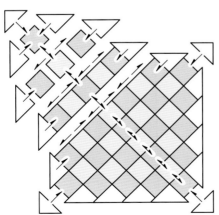

2 Trim the block to measure 11⅛" square, including seam allowances. Be sure to leave ¼" beyond the points of the dark squares. Make 25 blocks.

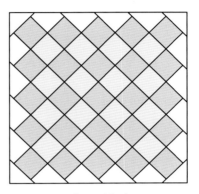

Trim ¼" from point.

Make 25 blocks,
11⅛" × 11⅛".

The Color Yellow

Though I never used much yellow in my quilts before, the pops of yellow in Checkerboard make the whole quilt sparkle and add a splash of warmth. You never know when you'll see something in a different way that changes how you think and feel about the world. It's exciting when you're inspired to try new things.

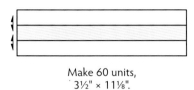

ASSEMBLING THE QUILT

1 Sew one pink 1½" × 11⅛" strip between two white 1½" × 11⅛" strips to make a sashing unit that measures 3½" × 11⅛". Make 60 sashing units.

Make 60 units,
3½" × 11⅛".

2 Join six pink 3½" squares and five sashing units, pressing away from the squares, to make a sashing row as shown in the assembly diagram below. Make six sashing rows that measure 3½" × 71⅝", including seam allowances.

3 Join five blocks and six sashing units, pressing toward the sashing units, to make a block row. Make five rows that measure 11⅛" × 71⅝", including seam allowances.

4 Sew the block rows and sashing rows together to complete the quilt top. It should measure 71⅝" square.

FINISHING THE QUILT

Visit ShopMartingale.com/HowtoQuilt for help with any of the following finishing techniques.

1 Layer and baste your quilt, and quilt by hand or machine. The quilt shown is machine quilted in a Baptist Fan design.

2 Using the pink print 2" × 42" strips, prepare binding; attach the binding to the quilt.

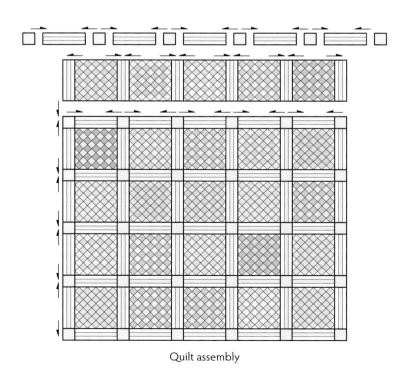

Quilt assembly

Pouch

Finished pouch: 4" × 8" × 1"

It's easy to scale the squares up or down to change the look. It's fun to sew a mere handful of squares into a larger piece of patchwork that you can cut up and turn into something useful. I arranged my squares in an alternating light/dark pattern, but anything goes.

MATERIALS

Yardage is based on 42"-wide fabric.

¼ yard *total* of assorted prints for bag front and back

⅛ yard of coordinating print for sides and zipper binding

⅜ yard of fabric for lining and interior binding

15" × 25" piece of ByAnnie's Soft and Stable bag batting*

Embroidery floss in a coordinating color for embellishing patchwork

Freezer paper or other paper for templates

1 zipper, 8" long

3" piece of ⅝"-wide lace for zipper tabs

1 charm for zipper pull (optional)

Fabric basting spray (optional)

*See "ByAnnie's vs. Batting" on page 77 to make use of traditional batting instead.

CUTTING

From the assorted prints, cut:
98 squares, 1½" × 1½"

From the coordinating print, cut:
1 strip, 1½" × 22¾"
2 strips, 1¼" × 8½"

From the lining fabric, cut:
1 piece, 11" × 12"
1 strip, 2" × 22¾"
4 bias strips, 1¼" × 16"
1 piece, 1¼" × 1½"

From the bag batting, cut:
1 piece, 11" × 12"
1 strip, 2" × 22¾"

MAKING THE PATCHWORK PARTS

Press seam allowances as indicated by the arrows in the illustrations or as otherwise stated.

1 Arrange the 98 print squares on point in diagonal rows as shown. Sew the squares together in diagonal rows and then sew the rows together to make a piece that measures approximately 11½" × 10½".

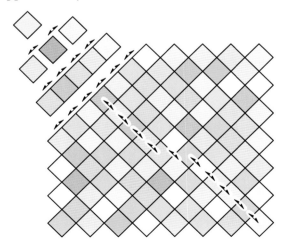

2 Use the patterns on pattern sheet 1 to make freezer-paper templates for the pouch bottom and top.

PERFECTLY PRETTY PATCHWORK

3 Place the templates on the patchwork and trace around them with a fabric marker. Trace the pouch bottom once and the pouch top twice. Don't cut out the pieces yet. Embroider a colonial knot (or French knot) at the intersection of each square within the traced areas. Refer to "Embroidery Basics" on page 78 for stitch details.

4 Place the 11" × 12" batting piece on the wrong side of the 11" × 12" lining piece, aligning the raw edges. Place the patchwork piece on top, right side up. Pin or spray baste the layers together and quilt by hand or machine. I outline quilted through each square, approximately ⅛" from the seams.

5 Place the templates for the top and bottom on the quilted piece within the traced lines and press or pin the templates to the patchwork. Cut along the edges of the paper. Cutting along the template's edge will ensure your pattern is accurate.

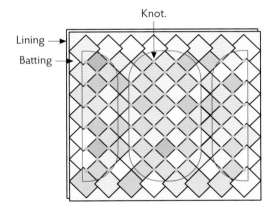

MAKING THE POUCH TOP

1 With right sides together, pin and sew a print 1¼" × 8½" strip to the straight edge of each pouch top to make a binding. Fold the binding over to the wrong side, turn under a ¼" seam allowance, and hand stitch the binding to the wrong side.

2 Lay the zipper right side up on a flat work surface. Lay one pouch top right side up, aligning the binding with the middle of the zipper teeth. Pin in place and hand stitch the zipper to the lining side with a backstitch, approximately ⅛" from the teeth. Then secure the loose edge of the zipper

tape to the lining with a hem stitch. Repeat to sew the other pouch top to the opposite side of the zipper.

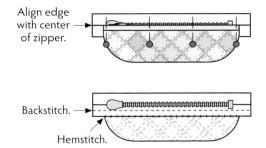

3 To make zipper tabs, cut the lace in half to make two 1½"-long pieces. Fold each piece of lace in half to measure ⅝" × ¾". Align the raw edges of the lace with each end of the zipper. Machine baste with a scant ¼" seam allowance, sewing with the patchwork side down so you can see the zipper teeth. Trim the zipper ends even with the patchwork.

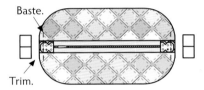

MAKING THE POUCH SIDES

1 Lay the lining 2" × 22¾" strip wrong side up with the 2"-wide batting strip on top. Add the print 1½" × 22¾" strip, right side up, on top. Spray or pin baste the layers together and quilt. I quilted five rows of topstitching along the length of the strip. Don't quilt into the seam allowances of the 1½" strip. Trim the batting and lining even with the print strip. To reduce bulk, trim the batting from the seam allowances.

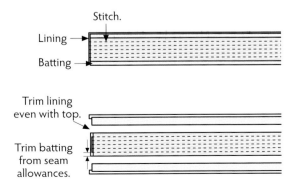

2 With right sides together, sew the two short ends of the gusset (pouch sides) together using a ¼" seam allowance. Trim the excess batting from the seam allowance.

3 Bind the seam allowance of the gusset with the 1¼" × 1½" rectangle of lining: Place the 1½" edge right sides together along the seam, aligning the raw edge with the raw edges of the seam allowances. Stitch along the seam over the previous stitching and then fold the binding over the seam allowances. Turn under ¼" and hand or machine stitch the binding to the lining. Fold the bound seam allowance to one side and hand stitch it to the gusset so that it's flat.

ASSEMBLING THE POUCH

1 Fold the pouch bottom in half in both directions and insert pins at each fold to mark the midpoints. In the same manner, mark the gusset with pins.

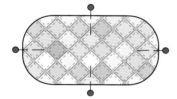

2 With right sides together, align the pins on one side of the gusset with the pins on the pouch bottom; pin all the way around. Sew the gusset to the pouch bottom.

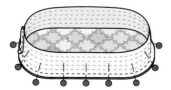

3 Open the zipper about halfway and repeat steps 1 and 2 to sew the pouch top to the gusset.

4 Join the 1¼" bias strips of lining fabric into one long length and press seam allowances open. Trim one end to a right angle, fold under ¼", and press. Press under ¼" along one long edge.

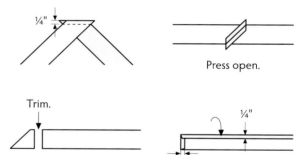

¼"

Press open.

Trim.

¼"

¼"

5 Beginning with the folded end, sew the bias strip to the inside seam allowances to make a single-fold binding as you did for the side seam. Trim the extra length, overlap the ends, and fold the binding over the seam allowances. Pin and hand stitch the binding to the lining. Bind both the bottom and top seam allowances in this manner.

6 Turn the pouch right side out through the zipper opening and press the seams to shape it. Optional: attach a charm to the zipper pull.

Dresden Plate

This sweet and versatile quilt motif has been, and continues to be, much adored by quilters throughout the ages. A Google search will prove that to you in seconds!

Mini-Quilt

Finished quilt: 34" × 34"
Finished block: 4" × 4"

How small is too small? I don't know, but I do know that these pretty 3" Dresden Plates are not too small to create a big impact. They're surrounded by an equally small—and equally delightful—Irish Chain setting.

MATERIALS

Yardage is based on 42"-wide fabric.

75 squares, 5" × 5", of assorted blue prints for blocks

⅜ yard of blue solid for blocks and inner border

1⅓ yards of white print for blocks

⅝ yard of blue print for border and binding

1⅛ yards of fabric for backing

40" × 40" piece of batting

Template material: plastic, freezer paper, or other paper

Fabric basting spray (optional)

CUTTING

Using the patterns on pattern sheet 2, make templates for the blade and circle.

From *each* 5" print square, cut:
4 blades using template A (300 total)
4 squares, 1" × 1" (300 total; 12 are extra)

From the blue solid, cut:
25 circles using template B
1 strip, 1½" × 42"; crosscut into 24 squares, 1½" × 1½"
4 strips, 1¼" × 42"; crosscut into:
    2 strips, 1¼" × 30"
    2 strips, 1¼" × 28½"

From the white print, cut:
4 strips, 5" × 42"; crosscut into 25 squares, 5" × 5"
10 strips, 1½" × 42"; crosscut into:
    96 rectangles, 1½" × 2½"
    96 rectangles, 1" × 1½"
5 strips, 1" × 42"; crosscut into 192 squares, 1" × 1"

From the blue print, cut:
4 strips, 2" × 42"
2 strips, 2½" × 34"
2 strips, 2½" × 30"

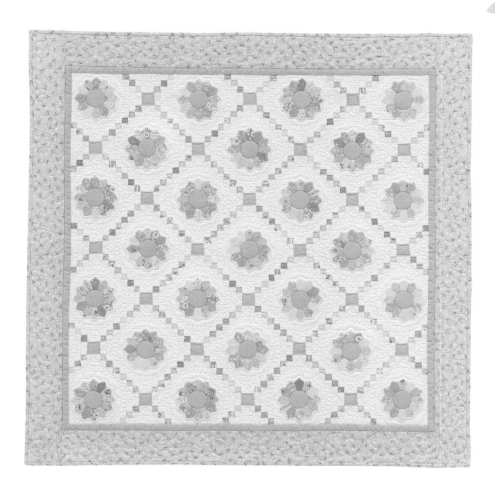

MAKING THE DRESDEN PLATE BLOCKS

Press seam allowances as indicated by the arrows in the illustrations or as otherwise stated.

1 Fold a blade in half lengthwise, right sides together. Sew across the wide end and trim the folded corner above the seam. Finger-press the seam open. Turn the blade right side out and use a slim Hera marker or other tool to turn the point so that it has a nice, sharp point; press. Make 300 blades.

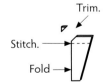

Make 300 units.

2 Choose 12 blades for one block. Place two blades right sides together and sew along one long side, backstitching at each end. Refer to "Helpful Hint" on page 50 for sewing tips. Repeat to sew the 12 blades together to make a Dresden plate. Make 25.

Stitch.

Make 25 units.

3 Prepare the blue solid circles for your preferred method of appliqué. For help with appliqué techniques, visit ShopMartingale.com/HowtoQuilt for free, downloadable instructions. Stitch a blue circle to the center of each Dresden plate from step 2.

4 Fold a white 5" square in half horizontally and vertically to find the center. Position and pin the Dresden plate in the center of the square. Appliqué it in place by hand or machine. Trim the block to measure 4½" square. Make 25 blocks.

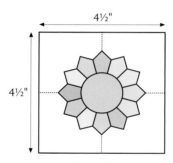

4½"

4½"

Appliqué placement

MAKING THE IRISH CHAIN BLOCKS

1 Arrange and sew two print and two white 1" squares together as shown to make a four-patch unit. The unit should measure 1½" square, including seam allowances. Make 96 four-patch units.

Make 96 units, 1½" × 1½".

2 Arrange and sew four print 1" squares, four white 1" × 1½" rectangles, and a blue solid 1½" square together to make a nine-patch unit. The unit should measure 2½" square, including seam allowances. Make 24 nine-patch units.

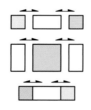

Make 24 units, 2½" × 2½".

Use Your Ruler

When sewing together very small pieces, a tiny variance in cutting or seam allowance can affect precision. Measure the four-patch and nine-patch units and trim, if necessary, before assembling the Irish Chain block.

3 Arrange and sew four four-patch units, one nine-patch unit, and four white 1½" × 2½" rectangles together as shown to complete the

block. It should measure 4½" square, including seam allowances. Make 24 Irish Chain blocks.

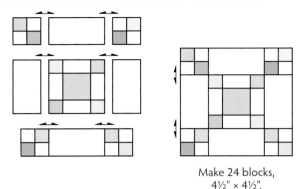

Make 24 blocks,
4½" × 4½".

ASSEMBLING THE QUILT TOP

1 Lay out the 25 Dresden Plate blocks and 24 Irish Chain blocks in seven rows of seven blocks each, alternating the blocks as shown below. Sew the blocks into rows and then sew the rows together. The quilt center should measure 28½" square, including seam allowances.

2 Sew the blue solid 1¼" × 28½" strips to the top and bottom of the quilt center. Sew the 1¼" × 30" strips to the sides.

3 Sew the blue print 2½" × 30" strips to the top and bottom of the quilt center. Sew the blue print 2½" × 34" strips to the sides. The quilt top should measure 34" square.

FINISHING THE QUILT

Visit ShopMartingale.com/HowtoQuilt for help with any of the following finishing techniques.

1 Layer and baste the quilt top, batting, and backing. Quilt by hand or machine. The quilt shown is machine quilted and features outline quilting around the appliquéd Dresden plates and a feather design in the background space. The border is quilted in swirls and feathers.

2 Using the blue print 2" × 42" strips, prepare binding; attach the binding to the quilt.

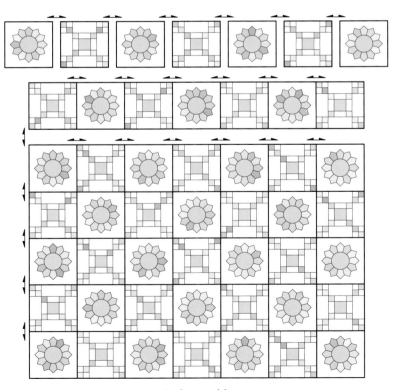

Quilt assembly

PERFECTLY PRETTY PATCHWORK

Purse

Finished purse: 8" × 8" × 2½"
Finished Dresden Plate: 6" diameter

The Dresden Plate is an adaptable design. The length of the blades can be adjusted to change the size of the block, and if you change the blade width, you can increase or decrease the number of blades needed. The center circle can also be made larger or smaller. Modifying any of these Dresden features will create a different appearance, giving your project a unique personality.

MATERIALS

Yardage is based on 42"-wide fabric.

20 squares, 3" × 3", of assorted blue prints for blades

1 square, 4" × 4", of light blue check for center circle

1 square, 10" × 10", of white dot print for purse front

1 yard of blue print for gusset, back, lining, and strap

10" × 44" piece of ByAnnie's Soft and Stable
    bag batting*

2 lobster claw clasps, ¾" wide

2 D-rings, ¾" wide

1 lightweight zipper, at least 12" long**

Template material: plastic, freezer paper,
    or other paper

Fabric basting spray (optional)

See "ByAnnie's vs. Batting" on page 77 if you prefer to use traditional batting.

**Choose a zipper color that matches or coordinates with the purse and handle fabric. If the zipper is longer than needed, it can be trimmed when inserting it.*

CUTTING

Using the patterns on pattern sheet 2, make templates for the blade and circles.

From *each* of the assorted blue prints, cut:
1 blade using template C (20 total)

From the light blue check, cut:
1 circle using template D

From the white dot print, cut:
1 circle, 8½" diameter, using template E

From the blue print, cut:
3 circles, 9" diameter, using template F
2 rectangles, 3½" × 13", for zipper gusset
2 rectangles, 3½" × 15", for gusset and gusset lining
2 rectangles, 2¼" × 3", for D-ring tabs
2 rectangles, 1¼" × 3", for binding gusset seams
2 bias strips, 1¼" × 28", for inner binding
1 strip, 3" × 42", for strap

From the bag batting, cut:
2 circles, 8" diameter, using template G
2 strips, 1¾" × 11¾", for zipper gusset
2 rectangles, ⅞" × 2", for D-ring tabs
1 strip, 3½" × 13½", for gusset bottom
1 strip, 1" × 41", for strap

MAKING THE PURSE FRONT AND BACK

1 Fold a blade shape in half lengthwise, right sides together. Referring to step 1 of "Making the Dresden Plate Blocks" on page 45, sew across the top edge and trim the corner seam allowance. Finger-press the seam open. Turn the blade right side out and use a slim Hera marker or other tool to turn the corner so it has a nice, sharp point. Make 20 blades.

2 Place two blades right sides together and sew along one long side, backstitching at both ends. Repeat to sew the 20 blades together to make a ring.

Helpful Hint

When sewing the blades together, start the seam ¼" below the top, backstitch to the top edge, and then sew back down the length of the blades. Reinforcing the top of the seams will prevent the plate from becoming distorted before you appliqué it. Starting ¼" from the edge will ensure the end threads are well hidden.

3 Prepare the blue check circle for your preferred method of appliqué. Visit ShopMartingale.com/HowtoQuilt for free, downloadable instructions if you need help with appliqué techniques. Stitch the circle to the center of the ring from step 2 to make a Dresden plate.

4 Fold the white dot circle in half horizontally and vertically to find the center. Position and pin the Dresden plate to the center of the circle for the purse front. Appliqué it in place by hand or machine.

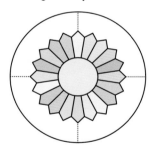

Appliqué placement

5 Place one blue lining circle wrong side up on your work surface and center a batting circle on top. Place the appliquéd purse front right side up on top. Pin or spray baste the three layers together. Quilt as desired. The purse shown is hand quilted with a grid of squares in the center circle. The blades

are outline quilted inside the pieces and around the outer edges. Trim the excess lining fabric even with the purse front.

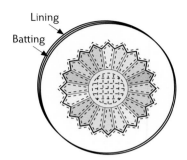

Lining

Batting

6 Repeat step 5 with the remaining circles for the purse back, the batting, and lining. Quilt a diagonal grid of squares or as desired. Trim the quilted piece using the 8½" template E circle.

INSERTING THE ZIPPER

1 Lay the blue print 3½" × 13" strips right sides together. Machine sew a long basting stitch through the middle. Fold each strip along the seam so that the wrong sides are together. Press.

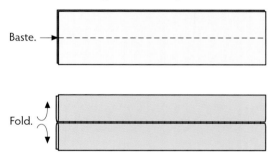

Baste. →

Fold.

2 Place the 1¾" × 11¾" batting strips inside the folds on both sides of the basted seam, keeping them centered along the length. Spray baste or pin the batting to the fabric.

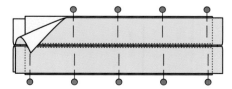

3 Place the piece flat on your work surface and lay the zipper, wrong side up, along the basted seam. The zipper teeth should nest along the seam. Pin the zipper in place and baste by hand.

Trimming a Zipper

If your zipper extends beyond the gusset, open the zipper halfway. Sew a few zigzag reinforcing stitches across the zipper teeth 12" from the zipper pull to create a new zipper stop. Then trim off the excess zipper. Stitch slowly—even by hand turning the flywheel—to avoid stitching into the zipper teeth.

4 Turn the piece right side up, and with a zipper foot on your sewing machine, sew ⅛" away from the basted center seam on each side. Be sure to change the stitch setting back to a regular stitch length.

5 With a regular presser foot, sew a second row of stitches on each side, about ¼" from the first stitching. Repeat to sew three more rows ¼" apart.

6 Trim the zipper gusset to measure 3" × 12¼", keeping the zipper centered. Baste along each end of the zipper to keep the edges together. Along the raw edges, trim ¼" from the batting only to minimize bulk in the seam allowances.

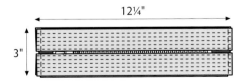

7 Carefully remove the basting stitches from the center seam to expose the zipper.

ADDING THE D-RINGS

1 Fold over ¼" along one long edge of a blue 2¼" × 3" rectangle and press. Lay a ⅞" × 2" batting rectangle on the wrong side. Wrap the fabric around the batting and fold so that the raw edge is covered by the folded edge. Press.

2 Topstitch three rows through the layers to make a tab for the D-ring. Make two tabs.

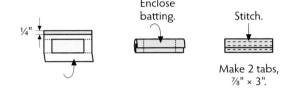

Make 2 tabs, ⅞" × 3".

3 Insert each tab into D-ring. Fold tab in half. Baste the ends together with a scant ¼" seam allowance.

Baste.

Make 2.

4 Open the zipper a few inches and center a tab on the right side of zipper gusset at each end. Pin and baste in place with a scant ¼" seam allowance.

Baste. 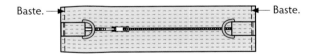 Baste.

MAKING THE BOTTOM GUSSET

1 Place a blue 3½" × 15" rectangle for the bottom gusset wrong side up and center the 3½" × 13½" batting strip on top. Add the remaining blue 3½" × 15" rectangle for the lining on top, right side facing up. Pin or spray baste the layers together. Quilt 10 rows of topstitching, ¼" apart, through the center. Leave ½" unquilted on each long side.

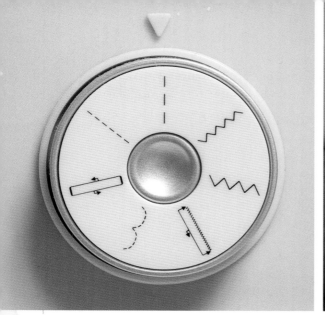

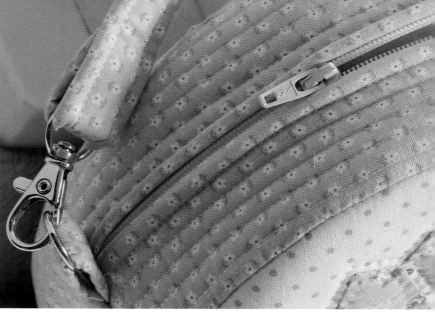

2 Trim the bottom gusset to measure 3" × 14", keeping the batting centered along the length. You should have ¼" beyond the batting on each 3" end for seam allowances. Then trim the excess batting from the ¼" seam allowance on the long sides to reduce bulk as you did for the zipper gusset.

COMPLETING THE GUSSET

1 Place the zipper gusset section on the bottom gusset, right sides together. Pin the short edges together and machine baste with a scant ¼" seam allowance. Repeat with the other end.

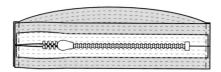

2 Test the fit of the gusset by pinning the gusset, right sides together, with the purse front. Pin all the way around. If the gusset is too big, take in one of the seams. If the gusset is too small, reduce the purse front with a very narrow trim around the entire circle. Repin the gusset. If you trim the purse front, trim the purse back to match. When the gusset fit is accurate, remove the pins and set aside the purse front.

3 Bind the seams of the gusset using the blue 1¼" × 3" rectangles. To bind the first seam,

place the zipper wrong side up. Place the 3" edge of the rectangle right sides together with the raw edges of the seam allowances. Sew along the previous stitching.

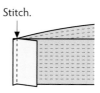
Stitch.

4 Fold the rectangle away from the zipper and over the seam allowance. Fold the raw edge of the binding rectangle over, wrong sides together, to meet the raw edge of the seam allowance. Then fold the binding over again so the seam allowance is completely covered. Hand or machine stitch the folded edge of the binding in place along the seam.

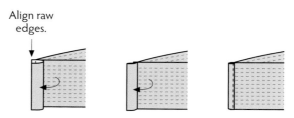
Align raw edges.

5 Press the bound seam allowances toward the purse bottom. Pressing in this direction will help the tab on the other side to point toward the zipper. Hand stitch the bound seam allowances to the gusset. Repeat steps 3–5 for the other seam.

PERFECTLY PRETTY PATCHWORK

ASSEMBLING THE PURSE

1 Fold the purse back circle in half in both directions and insert pins at each fold to mark the midpoints. In the same manner, mark the gusset midpoints with pins.

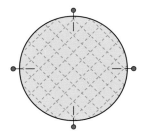

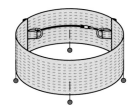

2 With right sides together, match the pins on one side of the gusset with the pins on the circle. Pin all the way around, inserting the pins so the gusset is on top and the circle is on the bottom. Sew together using a ¼" seam allowance.

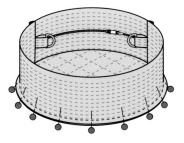

3 Make sure the zipper is open a few inches and repeat steps 1 and 2 with the purse front.

4 To make single-fold binding, turn under ¼" along one short edge of a blue 1¼" × 28" strip; press. Then fold under ¼" along one long edge; press.

5 Bind the inside seam allowances with the single-fold binding, stitching it by machine with a scant ¼". Trim the excess binding, fold the binding over the seam allowances, and then hand stitch the binding to the lining. Repeat for the other side.

6 Turn the purse right side out through the zipper opening and press the seams to shape the purse.

MAKING THE SHOULDER STRAP

1 Fold under ½" along one long edge of the blue 3" × 42" strip and press.

2 Center the 1" × 41" strip of batting on the wrong side of the strip. Fold under ½" on each short end of the fabric. Fold the long raw edge of the fabric over the batting and press. Then fold the remaining edge over and pin in place.

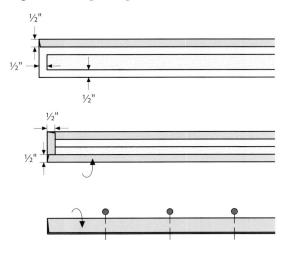

3 Sew two rows of topstitching along the length of the strap. Insert one end of the strap through the opening of a clasp. Fold back 1" and pin to the wrong side of the strap. Adjust length as desired and repeat for the other side. Hand stitch the end in place.

4 Attach the strap clasps to the D-rings.

Strips and Squares

Quilters are known for being thrifty and creative with leftover fabric scraps.
Sewing strips of varying widths together to form a block is a quick and
easy trick for getting the most out of a piece of fabric.

Quilt

Finished quilt: 74" × 74"
Finished block: 3½" × 3½"

Quilters love to showcase favorite prints. This design
combines blocks of scrappy strips with unpieced
squares of a pretty print, making it the quintessential
quilters' quilt!

MATERIALS

*Yardage is based on 42"-wide fabric. Fat eighths
measure 9" × 21".*

36 fat eighths (or 4½ yards total) of assorted light
   prints for blocks

3⅛ yards of medium- or large-scale pink floral for
   alternate blocks, border, and binding

4⅝ yards of fabric for backing

82" × 82" piece of batting

2 skeins of coordinating embroidery floss

CUTTING

From *each* of the assorted fat eighths, cut:
2 strips, 4" × 21"; crosscut *each* strip into:*
   3 rectangles, 1¾" × 4" (216 total)
   4 rectangles, 1½" × 4" (288 total)
   4 rectangles, 1¼" × 4" (288 total)
   3 rectangles, 1" × 4" (216 total)

From the pink floral, cut o*n the lengthwise grain*:
4 strips, 7½" × 70"

From the *remainder* of the pink floral, cut:
8 strips, 2" × 42"
65 squares, 4" × 4"

*The number of rectangles cut will be more than is
needed, to give flexibility in making the blocks.*

MAKING THE BLOCKS

Press seam allowances as indicated by the arrows in the illustrations.

Piece together four or more assorted 4" rectangles of varying widths until you have a block that's at least 4" square. Trim the block to measure 4" × 4", including seam allowances. Make 224 pieced blocks.

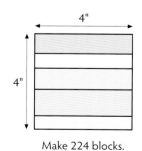

Make 224 blocks.

You Decide

The number of pieced blocks and solid squares are suggested guidelines only. If you're using scraps, make do with what you have and adjust the number of pieced blocks and squares as needed.

PERFECTLY PRETTY PATCHWORK

ASSEMBLING THE QUILT

1 Lay out the pieced blocks and the floral print squares in 17 rows of 17 blocks each. Alternate the orientation of the blocks so that some strips are vertical and some are horizontal. Place the unpieced squares randomly throughout the quilt. Sew the blocks and squares into rows, and then sew the rows together. The quilt center should measure 60" square, including seam allowances.

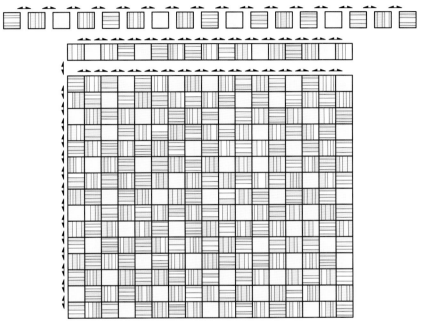

Quilt assembly

2 The borders are attached with the partial seam technique, and each border is the same length. Cut the four floral 7½" × 70" strips into four strips, 67" long.

3 Sew the first border to the right side of the quilt, but stop sewing approximately 7" before the bottom of the quilt center.

4 Add the next border to the top, sewing the complete seam. Work around the quilt in a counterclockwise direction. After the last

border is attached, sew the remaining seam of the first border. The quilt top should measure 74" square.

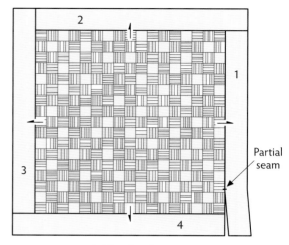

Adding borders

FINISHING THE QUILT

Visit ShopMartingale.com/HowtoQuilt for help with any of the following finishing techniques.

1 Layer and baste your quilt, and quilt by hand or machine. The quilt shown is quilted with an overall floral design in the center and continuous feathers in the border.

2 Using the floral 2" × 42" strips, prepare binding; attach the binding to the quilt.

3 Using two strands of floss, embroider a herringbone stitch on the seam between the patchwork and the borders. Refer to "Embroidery Stitches" on page 78 for stitch details.

3" × 10" rectangle of wool felt for pages

4" × 10" rectangle of fabric for page backing

4" × 12" rectangle of fusible web

Embroidery floss in a coordinating color

24" length of ribbon, ⅛" wide, for ties

10" length of double-edged lace, ⅝" wide,
    for pages (optional)

Label for back (optional)**

FriXion pen or other removable fabric marker

Pinking shears or scalloped scissors

Fabric basting spray (optional)

*As an alternative, you can use a square of fabric or
a leftover block from another project. The block or
square should measure or be trimmed to measure
3½" × 3½" for the larger needle book and 3" × 3" for
the smaller needle book, including seam allowances.*

**This can be a handmade label with the maker's
information (name, date, and place), or it can be a
charming purchased label. Add a quotation that you
love, or simply use a scrap of cherished fabric. It can
be any size as long as it fits on the needle book back.*

Needle Books

Finished needle books: 3½" × 3½" and 3" × 3"

In keeping with the "waste not, want not" quilting
tradition, a leftover block, or even just fabric scraps,
can be turned into a useful and pretty accessory,
like a sweet needle book. With additional leftover
pieces of lace and ribbons, a needle book can become
a visual delight. This will surely make quilters smile
when they're removing a slender needle to stitch
something pretty by hand.

MATERIALS FOR 1 NEEDLE BOOK
(Either Size)

Assorted scraps: 5 or 6 strips, 1" to 1¾" wide and
    4" long, for the 3½" needle book*
    OR 1 square, 3" × 3", for the 3" needle book*

5" × 5" square of coordinating print for exterior back

4" × 8" rectangle of light print for lining

1⅛" × 26" strip of coordinating print for binding

4" × 8" piece of batting

CUTTING FOR THE
3½" NEEDLE BOOK

From the exterior back fabric, cut:
1 rectangle, 3½" × 4¼"

From the lining fabric, cut:
1 rectangle, 3½" × 7¼"

From the batting, cut:
1 rectangle, 3½" × 7¼"

From the felt, cut:
3 rectangles, 3" × 3¼"

From page-backing fabric, cut:
3 rectangles, 3" × 3¼"

From the fusible web, cut:
3 rectangles, 3" × 3¼"

PERFECTLY PRETTY PATCHWORK

CUTTING FOR THE 3" NEEDLE BOOK

From the exterior back fabric, cut:
1 rectangle, 3" × 3¾"

From the lining fabric, cut:
1 rectangle, 3" × 6¼"

From the batting, cut:
1 rectangle, 3" × 6¼"

From the felt, cut:
2 rectangles, 2¾" × 3"

From the page-backing fabric, cut:
2 rectangles, 2¾" × 3"

From the fusible web, cut:
2 rectangles, 2¾" × 3"

MAKING THE BLOCK

Instructions are for one needle book. Press seam allowances as indicated by the arrows in the illustrations.

1 For the 3½" needle book, sew the assorted 4"-long strips together until you have a block that's at least 4" square. Trim the block to measure 3½" square.

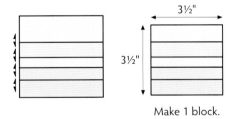

Make 1 block.

2 Embellish the block (or square for the 3" needle book) as desired with embroidery stitches or scraps of lace. The larger project shown is stitched along the seamlines with a herringbone stitch using a single ply of floss. Refer to "Embroidery Basics" on page 78 for stitch details.

ASSEMBLING THE NEEDLE BOOK

1 Sew the exterior-back rectangle to the front square, right sides together along one short edge, to make the exterior of the needle book.

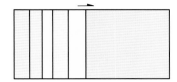

2 Lay the pieced unit, right side up, on the batting rectangle. Pin or spray baste the layers together and quilt by hand or machine. The projects shown are hand quilted. The pieced block features horizontal lines, parallel to the seam lines, while the plain square is quilted in a diagonal grid. Quilt the back the same as the front.

3 Make and add a label or other decorative element to the back, stitching it by hand or machine. The label can be centered or placed in a corner—it's up to you.

4 Place the lining rectangle onto the quilted exterior, wrong sides together. Pin and baste around the edges using a scant ¼" seam allowance.

5 Cut the ribbon in half to make two lengths, 12" long. Pin and baste the ribbons to the center of the short ends of the exterior.

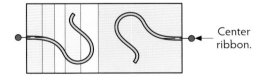

Center ribbon.

6 Using the 1⅛"-wide binding strip, prepare single-fold binding and attach the binding to all four edges, beginning on the back near the seam. The binding joining seam will be hidden when the book is "bound" with embroidery floss. Visit ShopMartingale.com/HowtoQuilt for free, downloadable instructions if you need help with binding techniques.

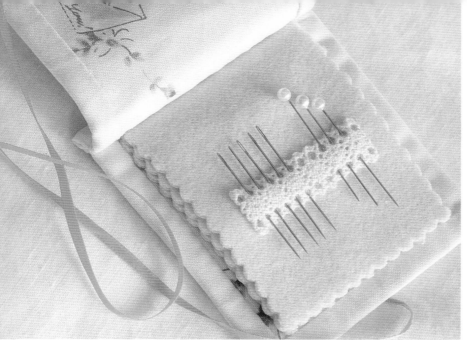

ADDING THE NEEDLE PAGES

1 Apply fusible web to the wrong side of each rectangle cut from the page-backing fabric. Remove the paper. Fuse the fabric to a felt page. Trim the page on both long edges and one short edge with pinking shears or decorative-edged scissors to measure 2¾" × 3" for the 3½" version or 2½" × 2¾" for the 3" version. Make three needle pages for the 3½" version and two for the 3" version.

2 To add lace to an interior page, cut a 2½" length for the larger book and a 2¼" length for the smaller book. Fold under and press the raw edges of the lace. Cut a ½"-wide piece of fusible web a little shorter than the lace and apply it to the wrong side. Position the lace onto the page and fuse in place. Hand sew the edges.

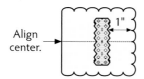

Align center.

3 Stack the pages and place them on the lining, keeping the straight edges of the pages aligned with the center of the book. There are three pages for the larger needle book and two pages for the smaller one.

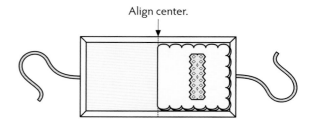

Align center.

4 Fold the book in half and secure the edges with pins or binding clips to keep them closed.

Embroidery Options

Whether you're a seasoned stitcher or just starting to explore the wonderful world of embroidery, this needle book offers the perfect opportunity to try out something new. The short seams provide enough space to create beautiful embellishments without taking too much time. It would be fun to practice an assortment of elaborate stitches, such as those featured on Victorian crazy quilts.

BINDING THE NEEDLE BOOK

1 To bind the book by hand, use a fabric marker to mark dots at ¼" intervals along the seam between the front and back.

2 Thread a needle with three plies of floss. (The illustration shows dark floss for clarity.) Knot the floss and insert the needle into the inner fold, bringing the needle out to the back at the binding seam. The knot will be hidden in the fold.

3 Insert the needle at the binding seam on the front about ¼" from the fold. Bring the needle out at the back and then loop the thread around the side and insert the needle at the base of the vertical stitch you just made. The stitch will be wrapped around the side horizontally.

 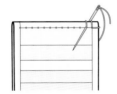

4 Insert the needle through to the front at the first ¼" mark, loop the thread over, and come back through at the same mark to make a vertical stitch. You'll be making a horizontal stitch on the back.

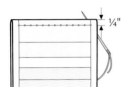 

5 Insert the needle from front to back at the next ¼" mark, making a horizontal stitch on the front. Bring the needle back to the front, looping the thread over the top. Insert the needle through the same point to make a vertical stitch.

 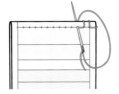

6 Insert the needle through to the front at the next ¼" mark, making a horizontal stitch on the back. Loop the thread over and come back through at the same mark to make a vertical stitch.

7 Repeat steps 5 and 6 across the needle book. When you reach the binding seam, loop the floss around the binding at the end and insert the needle on the other side. Stitch across the fold to make the horizontal stitches in the alternate spaces. Knot the thread and bury the knot in the layers. Trim the floss tail where it comes out of the fabric.

8 Add some needles to the pages of your book and enjoy.

Machine-Stitching Option

To bind the book by machine, start with the needle in the binding seam, ¼" from the folded edge. Backstitch to the outside edge, then stitch forward to the opposite end. Backstitch to the binding seam and tie off the thread.

Postage Stamp

The United States Postal Service issued stamps featuring the Basket block in 1978. While each stamp included just one Basket, the stamps were printed in sheets in groups of four, with the handles pointing inward. I just love this little quartet block.

Mini-Quilt

Finished quilt: 28" × 28"
Finished block: 6" × 6"

The beloved basket pattern, multiplied by four, creates the sweet Postage Stamp block. Repeating sets of four baskets form secondary design elements of straight and on-point squares. I love how simple blocks and a scrappy border combine to create a stunning whole.

MATERIALS

Yardage is based on 42"-wide fabric.

1 charm pack *OR* 36 squares, 5" × 5", of assorted prints for baskets and pieced border

1 yard of white solid for blocks and borders

⅓ yard of red print for binding

1 yard of fabric for backing

32" × 32" piece of batting

Template plastic or freezer paper

CUTTING

Using the pattern on page 68, make a template for the basket handle.

From *each* of the assorted 5" squares, cut:

1 square, 2⅞" × 2⅞"; cut in half diagonally to make 2 triangles (72 total). From *1* of the triangles, cut 1 handle using the template (36 total).

1 square, 1⅞" × 1⅞"; cut in half diagonally to make 2 triangles (72 total)

3 squares, 1½" × 1½" (108 total; 24 are extra)

From the white solid, cut:

2 strips, 3¼" × 28"

2 strips, 3¼" × 22½"

3 strips, 2⅞" × 42"; crosscut into 36 squares, 2⅞" × 2⅞". Cut in half diagonally to make 72 triangles.

5 strips, 1½" × 42"; crosscut into:

    2 strips, 1½" × 18½"

    2 strips, 1½" × 20½"

    72 squares, 1½" × 1½"

From the red print, cut:

4 strips, 2" × 42"

MAKING THE BLOCKS

Press seam allowances as indicated by the arrows in the illustrations or as otherwise stated. Visit ShopMartingale.com/HowtoQuilt for free, downloadable instructions if you need help with appliqué techniques.

1 Fold a white 2⅞" triangle in half and crease lightly to mark the center. Using the pattern on page 68, prepare a basket handle for your preferred method of appliqué. Fold a handle in half and mark the center

with a crease. Position and pin the basket handle on the white triangle and stitch in place using your preferred method of appliqué.

2 Sew the handle triangle to the matching print 2⅞" triangle. The unit should measure 2½" square, including seam allowances.

Make 1 unit,
2½" × 2½".

3 Sew a matching print 1⅞" triangle to a white 1½" square as shown. Repeat to make a second unit with the triangle facing the opposite direction. Sew the units to the basket square.

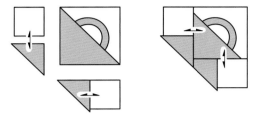

4 Sew a white 2⅞" triangle to the bottom of the unit to complete one basket. It should measure 3½" square, including seam allowances. Make 36 basket units.

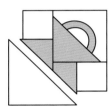 

Make 36 units,
3½" × 3½".

5 Sew four basket units together to make a block that measures 6½" square, including seam allowances. Make nine blocks.

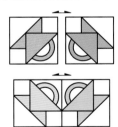 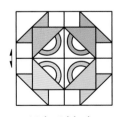

Make 9 blocks,
6½" × 6½".

ASSEMBLING THE QUILT

1 Arrange and sew the blocks together into three rows of three blocks each. Sew the rows together to complete the quilt center. It should measure 18½" square, including seam allowances.

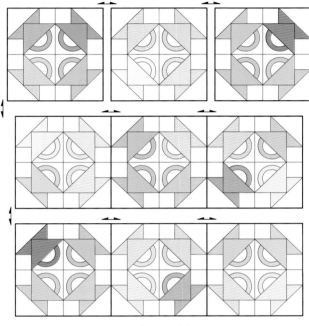

Quilt assembly

2 Sew the white 1½" × 18½" strips to the sides of the quilt center. Press the seam allowances toward the borders. Sew the white 1½" × 20½" strips to the top and bottom. Press the seam allowances toward the borders. The quilt center should measure 20½" square, including seam allowances.

3 Arrange and sew the print 1½" squares into two rows of 20 squares each and two rows of 22 squares each.

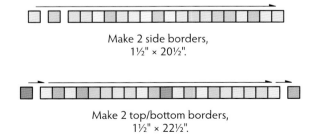

Make 2 side borders,
1½" × 20½".

Make 2 top/bottom borders,
1½" × 22½".

4 Sew the shorter pieced borders to the sides of the quilt first, then add the longer pieced borders to the top and bottom, pressing all seam allowances toward the white border. The quilt center should measure 22½" square, including seam allowances.

5 Sew the white 3¼" × 22½" strips to the sides of the quilt first, then sew the white 3¼" × 28" strips to the top and bottom, pressing all seam allowances toward the pieced border. The quilt top should measure 28" square.

FINISHING THE QUILT

Visit ShopMartingale.com/HowtoQuilt for help with any of the following finishing techniques.

1 Layer and baste your quilt, and quilt by hand or machine. The quilt shown is machine quilted with assorted leaves, petals, loops, and swirls.

2 Using the red 2" × 42" strips, prepare binding; attach the binding to the quilt.

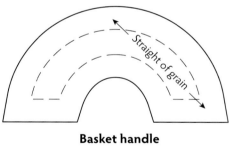

Basket handle
Cut 36.

Framed Quilt Blocks

Finished block: 9" × 9"

Place a quilt block in a frame and it becomes a piece of art. When the Postage Stamp block is enlarged and separated into four individual baskets, you'll have an instant set of coordinating images that can be arranged in any number of pleasing layouts.

MATERIALS FOR 4 FRAMED BLOCKS

4 squares, 12" × 12", of assorted blue prints
    for baskets
4 squares, 12" × 12", of assorted light prints for
    basket backgrounds
10" × 40" piece of batting
Template plastic or freezer paper
4 frames with 9" × 9" openings

CUTTING FOR 4 FRAMED BLOCKS

Using the pattern on pattern sheet 1, make a template for the basket handle.

From *each* of the assorted blue prints, cut:
1 square, 6⅞" × 6⅞"; cut in half diagonally to make
    2 triangles (8 total). From *1* of the triangles, cut
    1 handle using the template (4 total).
1 square, 3⅞" × 3⅞"; cut in half diagonally to make
    2 triangles (8 total)

From *each* of the assorted light prints, cut:
1 square, 6⅞" × 6⅞"; cut in half diagonally to make
    2 triangles (8 total)
2 squares, 3½" × 3½" (8 total)

From the batting, cut:
4 squares, 9½" × 9½"

3 Sew a matching blue 3⅞" triangle to a light 3½" square, pressing seam allowances open. Repeat to make a second unit with the triangle facing the opposite direction.

4 Sew the units from step 3 to the basket square as shown.

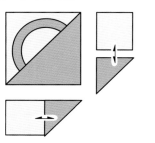
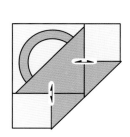

Make 1 unit.

5 Sew a light 6⅞" triangle to the bottom of the unit to complete the block. It should measure 9½" square, including seam allowances. Make four blocks.

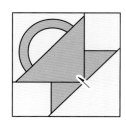

Make 4 blocks,
9½" × 9½".

MAKING THE BLOCKS

Press seam allowances as indicated by the arrows in the illustrations or as otherwise stated. Visit ShopMartingale.com/HowtoQuilt for free, downloadable instructions if you need help.

1 Fold a light 6⅞" triangle in half and crease lightly to mark the center. Using the pattern on pattern sheet 1, prepare a basket handle for your preferred method of appliqué. Fold the handle in half and mark the center with a crease. Position and pin the basket handle on the light triangle and stitch in place using your preferred method of appliqué.

2 Sew the appliquéd handle to the matching blue 6⅞" triangle, pressing away from the handle. The unit should measure 6½" square, including seam allowances.

Make 1 unit,
6½" × 6½".

FINISHING THE FRAMED BLOCKS

1 Layer a block right side up on a square of batting. Pin or spray baste the layers together and quilt by hand or machine. Repeat for each block. The blocks shown are outline quilted by hand, ¼" from both sides of each seam.

2 Insert the quilted blocks into the frames.

Flying Geese

Three sides, two sizes, one shape—that pretty much sums up the Flying Geese block,
one of the most widely used quilt motifs. It doesn't get any simpler or sweeter than that.

Baby Quilt

Finished quilt: 45½" × 49½"
Finished block: 5" × 10"

The scale of the Flying Geese blocks in this quilt offers
the perfect opportunity to showcase your favorite
fabric prints with big impact—and minimal sewing.
The large panels of the quilt give you a chance to use a
special fabric or a fabulous large-scale print that you
don't want to cut up in small pieces.

MATERIALS

Yardage is based on 42"-wide fabric.

9 squares, 12" × 12", of assorted red prints for blocks

½ yard of white print for blocks

1¾ yards of large-scale red print for panels
   and binding

3 yards of fabric for backing

52" × 56" piece of batting

2¾ yards of double-edged lace trim, ⅝" wide

CUTTING

From *each* of the 9 red print squares, cut:
1 square, 11¼" × 11¼"; cut into quarters diagonally
   to make 4 triangles (36 total; 27 are extra)

From the white print, cut:
2 strips, 5⅞" × 42"; crosscut into 9 squares,
   5⅞" × 5⅞". Cut in half diagonally to make
   18 triangles.

**From the large-scale red print, cut *on the
lengthwise grain*:**
1 panel, 30" × 45½"*
1 panel, 10" × 45½"*

**From the *remainder* of the large-scale
red print, cut:**
5 strips, 2" × 42"

**These panels can be slightly wider or narrower,
depending on the width of your fabric after removing
selvages. Just be sure each one is 45½" long.*

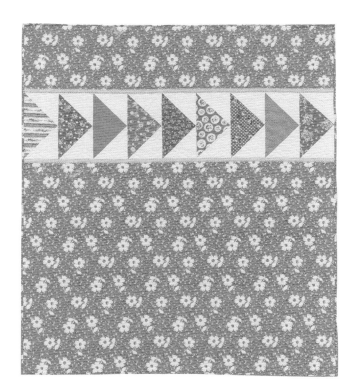

ASSEMBLING THE QUILT

1 Sew the blocks into a row, pressing the seam allowances toward the base of each triangle. The row should measure 10½" × 45½".

2 Sew the 10" × 45½" panel to the top of the geese row and the remaining panel to the bottom. The quilt top should measure 45½" × 49½".

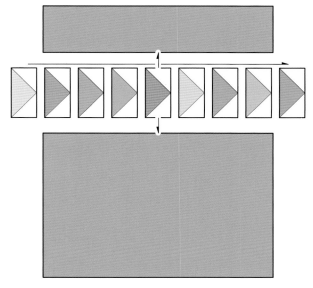

Quilt assembly

MAKING THE BLOCKS

Press seam allowances as indicated by the arrows in the illustrations.

Sew a white triangle to each short side of a red triangle to make a Flying Geese block. The block should measure 5½" × 10½", including seam allowances. Make nine blocks.

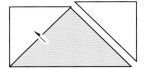 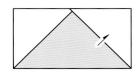

Make 9 blocks,
5½" × 10½".

FINISHING THE QUILT

Visit ShopMartingale.com/HowtoQuilt for help with any of the following finishing techniques.

1 Layer and baste your quilt, and quilt by hand or machine. The quilt shown is machine quilted with looping vines, leaves, flowers, and tendrils.

2 Measure the width of the quilt and cut two lengths of lace to that measurement. Sew a length of lace by hand or machine along the top and bottom of the Flying Geese row.

3 Using the red 2" × 42" strips, prepare binding; attach the binding to the quilt.

PERFECTLY PRETTY PATCHWORK

Zippered Pouch

Finished pouch: Approximately 7" × 4½" × 2"
Finished block: ⅞" × 1¾"

To a non-quilter, this little pouch features a striking geometric design. To a quilter's eye, however, the Flying Geese motif is unmistakable. Reducing the size of the block allows for a little flock of five baby geese. Does that mean we can call them flying goslings?

MATERIALS

Fat quarters measure 18" × 21"; fat eighths measure 9" × 21".

4" × 7" piece of white solid for blocks

10 scraps, at least 2" × 2", of assorted red prints for blocks

1 fat eighth of white print for pouch

1 fat eighth of red-and-white print for lining

4" × 6" piece of red print #1 for pouch bottom

1 fat quarter of red print #2 for binding

Template material: plastic, freezer paper, or other paper

9" × 21" piece of ByAnnie's Soft and Stable bag batting*

1 zipper, 8" long

12" length of lace, ⅜" wide

1 charm for zipper pull (optional)

Fabric basting spray (optional)

*See "ByAnnie's vs. Batting" on page 77 to make use of traditional batting instead.

CUTTING

Using the patterns on pattern sheet 1, make templates for the pouch front, back, and bottom.

From the white solid, cut:
2 squares, 3" × 3"; cut into quarters diagonally to make 8 triangles (3 are extra)

From *each* red scrap, cut:
1 square, 1¾" × 1¾"; cut in half diagonally to make 2 triangles (20 total; 10 are extra)

From the white print, cut:
1 pouch front
1 pouch front reversed
1 pouch back

From red print #1, cut:
1 pouch bottom

From red print #2, cut:
1¼" × 20" bias strip

From the lining fabric, cut:
2 pouch backs
1 pouch bottom

From the batting, cut:*
2 pouch backs
1 pouch bottom

*Cut the batting pieces without seam allowances to minimize bulk.

MAKING THE POUCH FRONT, BACK, AND BOTTOM

Press seam allowances as indicated by the arrows in the illustrations or as otherwise stated.

1 Sew different-print red triangles to the short sides of a white solid triangle to make a Flying Geese block. The block should measure 1⅜" × 2¼", including seam allowances. Make five blocks.

Make 5 blocks,
1⅜" × 2¼".

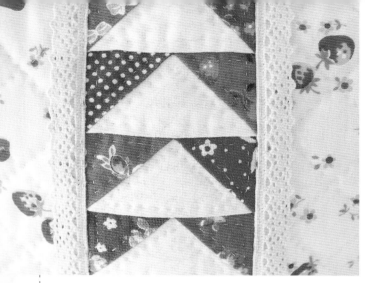

2 Sew the blocks together into a row. The row should measure 2¼" × 4⅞", including seam allowances.

3 Sew the white pouch front and pouch front reversed to each side of the patchwork row.

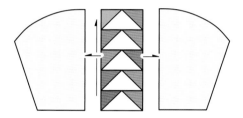

4 Layer the pieced front on top of a pouch back batting piece. Pin or spray baste the layers together and quilt as desired. The pouch shown is hand quilted in a diagonal grid along the sides. The Flying Geese row is outline quilted. The batting does not include seam allowances to minimize bulk in the seams. Be sure it's centered on the pieced front.

5 Sew a 4¾" length of lace to each side of the patchwork row.

6 Repeat step 4 with the white pouch back and remaining batting.

7 Repeat step 4 with the red #1 pouch bottom and batting.

ASSEMBLING THE POUCH

1 Lay the pouch front and back right sides together and sew the side seams. Press the seam allowances open.

2 With pins, mark the center of the front and back along the bottom edge and place pins at the side seams. Fold the pouch bottom in half in both directions and insert pins at each fold to mark the midpoints. With the pouch inside out, pin the bottom to the front and back, right sides together and matching the pins. Sew the pieces together.

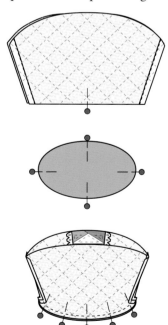

PERFECTLY PRETTY PATCHWORK

3 Repeat steps 1 and 2 with the three lining pieces.

4 Turn the pouch right side out and the lining inside out. Insert the lining into the pouch and baste them together around the top edge, by machine or by hand, with a scant ¼" seam allowance.

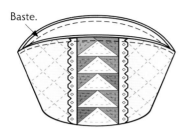

Baste.

5 Using the red print #2 bias strip, press under ¼" along one long edge. Sew the flat edge of the strip to the top edge of the pouch. Fold the strip over to the inside of the pouch and hand stitch the binding to the inside.

6 Turn the pouch inside out. Open the zipper and pin it in place along the top of the pouch. Hand stitch the zipper to the pouch using a backstitch. Then secure the edges of the zipper tape to the lining with a hemstitch. Make sure the stitches don't go through to the right side of the pouch.

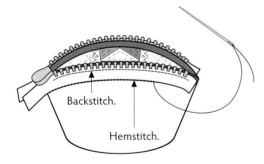

Backstitch.

Hemstitch.

7 Turn the pouch right side out and press the seams to shape it. Optional: attach a charm to the zipper pull.

By Annie's vs. Batting

For many of the dimensional projects in this book, I've used ByAnnie's Soft and Stable, a product designed specifically for purses, tote bags, and similar items. It's a bag batting that will give your projects a firm, crisp shape. You may not have ByAnnie's Soft and Stable on hand (yet!), and you may have plenty of batting scraps in your sewing room that you'd like to put to good use. In that case, you have the option of using regular batting in combination with fusible interfacing if you prefer.

When using regular batting, I pair it with a medium-weight fusible interfacing. Simply fuse the interfacing to the quilt batting, following the manufacturer's instructions. Then cut the batting as directed in the project instructions.

There are times when you may prefer the batting option as well. It will give a softer, "slouchy" appearance to a bag, tote, or pouch. You can use either option, depending on what type of finish you would like, what products you have on hand, and what is more readily available.

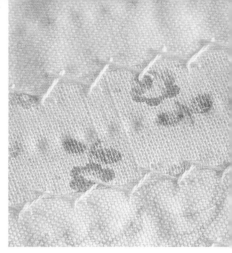

Embroidery Basics

Embroidery is one of my passions, and naturally I've included some embroidery on the projects in this book. Here I'll cover the basics of what you'll need to complete any of these projects, and hopefully it will inspire you to seek out other embroidery projects and learn more stitches.

SUPPLIES

These are the supplies you'll need for embroidery.

Embroidery floss. When it comes to floss, you get what you pay for. Cheap floss tangles and knots easily and will quickly lead to frustration. Spending a little more on a quality brand will make your stitching an enjoyable task with a beautiful finish. I prefer Cosmo and DMC brands. Floss is six-stranded; project instructions specify how many strands or plies to use.

Hoop. A hoop is used to help maintain tension in the fabric to prevent puckering while stitching. Some stitchers always use a hoop, while others never use one. I like to use a hoop for stab stitches, but no hoop for continuous stitches.

Marking tool. Temporary fabric markers have improved significantly since they first hit the market. I like to use a FriXion erasable fabric pen because the ink disappears with the heat from an iron. For a permanent marker, the Pigma Micron pen in a fine .005 tip, or a larger .01 tip, works well and comes in many colors. If you mark with tiny dots to create

your stitch guides rather than drawing solid lines, the stitching will cover the marks.

Needles. A good embroidery needle has an eye that's large enough to thread six strands of floss and has a sharp tip. These needles are available in different lengths. If you're new to embroidery, look for a variety pack so you can try them out and decide what's most comfortable for your hand.

Scissors. Choose a pair designed for embroidery—small, with sharp tips. I like spring-loaded thread snips; they're quick to pick up and get the job done.

TRANSFERRING DESIGNS ONTO FABRIC

There are many ways to transfer an embroidery design onto fabric. The easiest method for small projects is to use a light box or a sunny window. Place the pattern and then the fabric on the surface and trace the pattern onto the fabric using a marking tool.

EMBROIDERY STITCHES

Embroidery stitches can be classified as one of two types: stab or continuous. Stab stitches are made by passing the needle through the fabric in one direction at a time, such as the colonial or French knot. Continuous stitches are completed by passing the needle through the fabric from front to back to front in one movement, such as the herringbone and stem stitch.

They make your work look extra special, but these embroidery stitches aren't tricky at all. If you've never tried them before, you'll have these stitches perfected in no time.

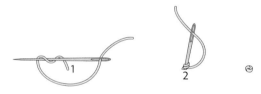

Colonial knot

French knot

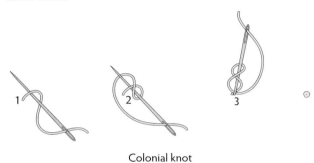

Herringbone stitch

Stem stitch
(Outline stitch)

Acknowledgments

These are some of the manufacturers, suppliers, and retailers whose products I enjoyed using while making the projects in this book.

Bunny's Designs, LLC
Etsy.com/FabricSupply

ByAnnie Soft and Stable bag batting
ByAnnie.com

Hollyhill Quilt Shoppe & Mercantile
HollyHillQuiltShoppe.com

Moda Fabrics
ModaFabrics.com

Olfa
Olfa.com/craft

Soak
SoakWash.com

Spring Promenade
Etsy.com/SpringPromenade

Sunny Day Supply
SunnyDaySupply.com

Special Thanks

Heather Tomlinson, thank you for letting me talk through design decisions with you, for offering your valued opinions, and for all your amazing stunt sewing.

A heartfelt thanks to Annie at Pinks and Needles for lending her incredible talent to creating the sweetest decorative pin toppers for my book. Check out her work at etsy.com/shop/PinksAndNeedles.

About the Author

Kristyne was born a maker. Her earliest memories include making craft projects of almost every description, including pom-poms, needlepoint, embroidery, macramé, decoupage, paint-by-numbers, friendship bracelets, and countless art kits that found their way into her hands.

She eventually fell hardest in love with making things out of fabric—pretty fabric in coordinating prints, if possible. Although she spent her high school and university years making garments that often didn't fit quite right, her love of fabric never waned. When introduced to quilting in 1985, she knew she'd found her passion. She hasn't stopped quilting since.

Her formal education gave her the skills to become a technical writer, which is her full-time career. She also uses her quilting experience and writing skills to design and publish quilt and sewing patterns as well as to teach quilting and sewing. Kristyne loves to share her passion and knowledge with the students in her classes.

Most recently, she spent four years taking night classes to earn a graphic-design certificate, which she's put to good use fulfilling her dream of becoming a fabric designer.

What's next? Who knows! Only one thing is certain . . . she'll be making.